SCIENCE AND FAITH

A New Introduction

John F. Haught

PAULIST PRESS
New York / Mahwah, NJ

Chapter 12 is adapted from "Theology after Contact: Religion and Extraterrestrial Intelligent Life," by John F. Haught, originally published in *Cosmic Questions*, New York Academy of Sciences Press, 2001. Used by permission.

Cover design by Sharyn Banks
Book design by Lynn Else

Library of Congress Cataloging-in-Publication Data

Haught, John F.
    Science and faith : a new introduction / John F. Haught.
        p. cm.
    Includes index.
    ISBN 978-0-8091-4806-6 (alk. paper) — ISBN 978-1-58768-085-4 1. Religion and science. I. Title.
    BL240.3.H39 2013
    201'.65—dc23

                                                            2012035899

Published by Paulist Press
997 Macarthur Boulevard
Mahwah, New Jersey 07430

www.paulistpress.com

Printed and bound in the
United States of America

Contents

Introduction

By the beginning of the twenty-first century, scientists had determined that the physical universe is about 13.7 billion years old. The human imagination cannot comprehend such an expanse of time, but try this experiment. Imagine the cosmic story as being told in thirty big books. Each book is 450 pages long, and each page stands for one million years in the story. The cosmos begins with the Big Bang on page 1 of volume 1. Then the next twenty-one volumes tell only about lifeless and mindless physical events. Clearly life was not in a hurry to come into the universe. The solar system appears around the beginning of volume 21, between 4 and 5 billion years ago. In volume 22, 3.8 billion years ago, the first sparks of life begin to glow on Earth. Still, life remains relatively simple, mostly single celled, until around the end of volume 29. At this point the famous Cambrian Explosion takes place, between 500 and 600 million years ago. During the Cambrian period, over a span of several million years, life "suddenly" begins to become much more complex than before. Dinosaurs appear a little after the middle of volume 30, and they go extinct on page 385.

Not until the last sixty-five pages of volume 30 do mammals begin to flourish on a large scale, evolving into many different species at a relatively accelerated pace. The first monkeys appear around 35 million years ago. Hominids start showing up during the last four or five pages of volume 30, but anatomically modern humans don't appear until roughly the bottom fifth of the very last page of the last volume. This is when reflective thought, ethical aspiration, and religious restlessness finally arrive, at least in our terrestrial precincts.[1]

If you're a scientifically educated person today, maybe you're already wondering whether this story has a point, a goal, a meaning. Is there some narrative thread that ties together what's going on in volume 1 with what's happening on page 450 of volume 30—and any

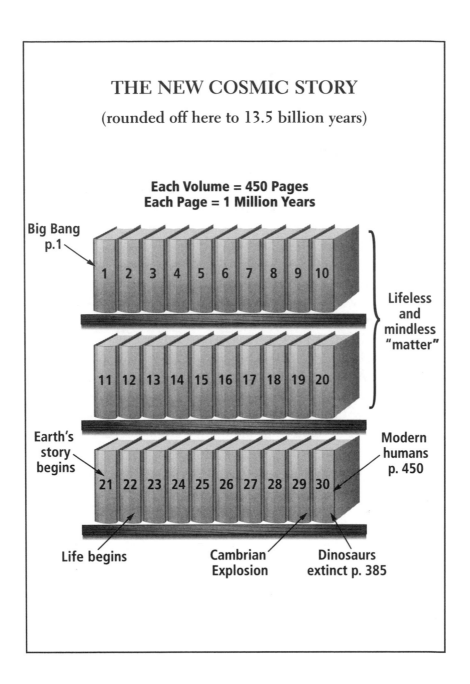

THE NEW COSMIC STORY

(rounded off here to 13.5 billion years)

Each Volume = 450 Pages
Each Page = 1 Million Years

Big Bang
p.1

1 2 3 4 5 6 7 8 9 10

11 12 13 14 15 16 17 18 19 20

Lifeless
and
mindless
"matter"

Earth's
story
begins

Modern
humans
p. 450

21 22 23 24 25 26 27 28 29 30

Life begins

Cambrian
Explosion

Dinosaurs
extinct p. 385

future volumes yet to be written? Does the whole set of books make any kind of overall sense?

Religions have been the main way in which most people have traditionally tried to make sense of what's going on in the world. But what sense are religious believers today going to make of the new cosmic story? Does the story have any religious meaning at all? Currently many sincere seekers see no special meaning and no overarching significance in the new scientific story of the universe. For some there is an irresolvable contradiction between the natural sciences and religious beliefs. Some traditionally religious believers find the new scientific story of the universe strange and disturbing, so they reject cosmology and evolutionary biology for making the world look so different from the one they have read about in their holy books. Other people of faith fully accept the new cosmic story as interesting and true, but they consider it theologically inconsequential. For them science raises no really new questions. And, finally, there are theologically interested people who find in the new cosmic story an opportunity to think new thoughts about God, human destiny, and what the universe is all about.

However, is science compatible with religious faith? Doesn't science rule out the existence of a personal God? After Darwin, can anyone honestly believe in divine providence? Do miracles really happen? Was the universe created or did it "just happen"? Isn't life reducible to chemistry? Is your mind anything more than your brain? Can't science now explain morality, and can't we be good without God? Are human beings special in the vast universe? Is there life after death? Does the universe have a purpose? And what, if anything, would it mean theologically if we eventually discover extraterrestrial life and intelligence?

This book lays out three distinct ways in which people who have been exposed to science are now responding to the questions just listed. The first kind of response claims that the natural sciences and religious faith are mutually exclusive. This is the *conflict* position. Its representatives include two main subgroups: (1) skeptics who believe that the natural sciences have made all religious claims unbelievable, and (2) people of faith who refuse to accept certain scientific ideas such as Big Bang cosmology and biological evolution.

However, in the present book *conflict* refers only to scientific skeptics, those who claim that scientific method and discoveries now make religious faith and theology obsolete. Representatives of the conflict approach include the so-called New Atheists: Richard Dawkins, Daniel Dennett, Sam Harris, and Christopher Hitchens. The New Atheists' recently popular publications may be the loudest expression so far of the belief that modern science makes the existence of God inconceivable for reasonable people. Because of their prominence in recent cultural and intellectual conversations, it is especially—though not exclusively—the New Atheists' voices that express the conflict position in these pages. Their opposition to "faith" might well be called "contempt," but most scientific skeptics do not share the New Atheists' venom and loathing of belief in God. Nevertheless, what they do generally share with the New Atheists is an unquestioning trust that science alone can lead the human mind to truth.

A second type of response to the set of questions listed claims that science and faith are each concerned with different levels or dimensions of reality. Science and theology, according to this approach, ask completely different kinds of questions, and so it makes no sense to place them in competition with each other. The *contrast* approach, as we call it, maintains that there can be no real conflict between the claims of natural science and those of faith and theology. Contrast insists that faith and science are not competing for some common goal, so they can't come into conflict with each other. Maybe you're inclined to follow this approach. If so, you're not alone.

A third approach is that of *convergence*. It might also be called "consonance," "cooperation," "contact," or "conversation." Convergence agrees with the contrast approach that religious faith and natural science are distinct ways of understanding the world, but it argues that the two inevitably interact. Convergence promotes this interaction. Its objective is to arrive at a synthesis in which both science and faith keep their respective identities while still relating closely to each other in a shared pursuit of intelligibility and truth. Convergence assumes that scientific discoveries matter to faith. In other words, scientific findings can make a significant difference in how we think about God and the meaning of our lives. Convergence wagers that science and faith, as long as they are not confused with each other, can together contribute to a richer view of reality than either can achieve on its own.

Each of the following chapters illustrates how the three approaches — conflict, contrast, and convergence — respond to the questions listed.

WHAT IS FAITH?

Instead of trying to relate science to the whole complex world of religions — an impossible task — our focus is on those religious traditions that profess *faith* in God and that interpret this faith in the form of what is known as "theology." Most readers, one may assume, already know something about natural science, but what about "faith" and "theology"? In this book the terms *faith* and *theology* refer to theistic belief and thought. "Theism" is religious belief in the one personal God associated with the Abrahamic religions, Judaism, Christianity, and Islam. These traditions differ considerably from one another, but they are all monotheistic, professing belief in only one God. And they all claim to be descendents of Abraham, whom we meet first in the Book of Genesis in the Bible. Biblical scholars generally agree that a figure named Abram (later called Abraham) lived in the ancient Near East during the early second millennium BCE. Judaism, Christianity, and Islam all profess faith in what they take to be Abraham's God.

The Abrahamic God's most characteristic attribute, as depicted in the Bible, is that of making and keeping promises. This is a God who can always be counted on to bring about a new future even when it seems there are only dead ends. Abraham's God, whom the ancient Hebrew people referred to as "Yahweh," and Muslims later as "Allah," is also said to be the creator and sustainer of the universe. Theistic faiths believe that God compassionately saves those who are lost, seeks justice for the poor and oppressed, and forgives those who have gone astray. Each monotheistic tradition adds its own nuances to this shared understanding of God. However, the present book speaks of God in a sense generic enough that people in all three Abrahamic traditions may enter into the conversations outlined in each of the following chapters.

It is of great significance to Jews and Muslims, and not just Christians, that since the beginning of the modern world many educated people have wondered whether faith in the God of Abraham is compatible with the natural sciences. Perhaps you too, at least at times, have harbored a similar suspicion. Are the natural sciences compatible with belief in the existence of the promising, loving, creative, personal, and redemptive deity that the "God-religions" profess to worship? Under the heading of "faith," the following conversations make reference also to the large body of theoretical and philosophical reflections on God commonly known as "theology." Do you, or do you not, think there is still space for a plausible theology in the age of science? This book lays out succinctly three main options for you to consider as you reflect on this question.

In broader conversations on religion and science it is also appropriate to talk about Buddhism, Hinduism, Taoism, and other great traditions. However, the focus of the present book is theological: Do the natural sciences rule out the personal God of Judaism, Christianity, and Islam? One might also understand religion broadly as "a sense of mystery." Having a sense of mystery is an important aspect of all religious awareness. But "mystery" is too vague an idea for the conversation outlined here. Moreover, having a sense of mystery is hardly controversial to many scientific skeptics, and it seldom provokes significant protests from scientifically educated people, including atheists. Even Albert Einstein, who rejected the idea of a personal God, confessed to being a religious man because of his appreciation of the incomprehensible mystery of the universe. Einstein, however, insisted that the idea of a personal, responsive God who answers prayers is incompatible with science. If the deity that Jews, Christians, and Muslims believe in really exists, Einstein thought, then this God could break or interrupt the changeless laws of nature anytime it seemed suitable. However, because science depends on the assumption that the laws of nature are unbreakable, Einstein claimed that belief in a personal God is incompatible with science.

Introduction

Perhaps your own scientific learning has already turned you away from association with faith and theology. Maybe, like the New Atheists and other contemporary skeptics, your scientific education has estranged you from your former beliefs. Or you may have found that modern and contemporary scientific discoveries make the idea of God more inviting and interesting than ever. Or you may be undecided about the whole business. Whatever your thoughts are at present, it will not hurt to look carefully at each of this book's three ways of understanding theistic faith in the age of science.

* * *

Author's note: The present book takes up some of the issues treated in my earlier book *Science and Religion: From Conflict to Conversation*. However, this is a different kind of work, a complete overhauling and not a mere revision of the older. It introduces new questions and drops others. Several chapter titles, definitions, citations, and occasional requisite phrasing used in the earlier book may appear here, but the content, conversational style, and overall organization of the material are new. Here, for example, the focus is on "faith" and "theology," rather than on the vaguer notion of "religion." This work is a product also of my growing interest in the "new cosmic story" and the "drama" of life. The material also reflects my more recent involvement in numerous conversations on the question of evolution and faith, as well as my recent study of the New Atheism. It deals in an abbreviated way with ideas presented in more detail in intervening books such as *Making Sense of Evolution: Darwin, God and the Drama of Life* (Westminster John Knox Press, 2010); *God and the New Atheism: A Critical Response to Dawkins, Harris and Hitchens* (Westminster John Knox Press, 2008); *God after Darwin: A Theology of Evolution* (Westview Press, 2000); and *Is Nature Enough? Meaning and Truth in the Age of Science* (Cambridge University Press, 2006). The reader is referred to these works for lengthier discussion of the topics outlined in the following chapters.

Here the treatment is also sparer and more pointed. *Science and Faith* is less an exposition than a provocation. It is an invitation to the reader to participate immediately, and perhaps even enthusiastically, in one of the most important conversations of our time. To this end I try here to make the whole conversation of faith and science accessible to a wider variety of potential readers than my earlier books may have permitted.

CHAPTER 1

Is Faith
Opposed to Science?

When we hear the words science and faith we immediately think of the stormy history of their relationship. But faith's encounter with science is not one of unceasing warfare. Keeping in mind that by "faith" this book means belief in the personal, responsive God of the Abrahamic religious traditions (Judaism, Christianity, and Islam), here again are the three main ways in which people who take science seriously relate it to the world of faith:

1. *Conflict:* Science and faith are opposed and irreconcilable.
2. *Contrast:* Science and faith are distinct, but they are not opposed to each other. No conflict can exist between faith and science since they each respond to radically different questions. There is no real competition between them, so there can be no real conflict.
3. *Convergence:* Science and faith are distinct because they ask different kinds of questions, but they may still interact fruitfully. Convergence tries to move beyond both conflict and contrast to a richer and more nuanced perspective, one that allows ample room for an ongoing conversation between science and faith. It focuses especially on the theological implications of the new cosmic story sketched in the introduction. Let us now examine each approach in more detail.

CONFLICT

Many educated people today have no doubt that faith is irreconcilable with science. For instance, Jerry Coyne, an evolutionist at the University of Chicago, believes that Charles Darwin's theory of evolution has demolished the idea of God once and for all. Contemporary best-selling authors Richard Dawkins, Sam Harris, Christopher Hitchens, and Daniel Dennett, known as the "New Atheists," agree. If you are a scientist, they declare, you cannot honestly believe in God. If you still believe in God in the age of science you are simply foolish. Faith, these skeptics insist, is "belief without evidence." You cannot demonstrate the truth of faith scientifically, so get rid of it. People of faith can provide no factual "evidence" of God's existence. Neither the five senses nor scientific instruments have ever detected the slightest trace of God. Faith is mere fiction and theology a waste of time.[1]

According to the conflict position, both historical investigation and philosophical reflection demonstrate that faith is opposed to science. Historically, simply recall the Catholic Church's prosecution of Galileo in the seventeenth century for teaching that the Earth revolves around the sun. And look at the opposition by Christians and Muslims to Darwin's evolutionary theory even today. Since so many believers in God have resisted the findings of astronomy, physics, and biology, how can one avoid the conclusion that faith is inherently hostile to science?

Philosophically, according to conflict, the problem is that beliefs about God are experimentally untestable. They do not lend themselves to the rigors of public examination, whereas science has to submit its ideas to open criticism and ongoing experimentation. If careful observation shows a scientific hypothesis to be mistaken, scientists willingly modify or discard it and try out new ones. Faith, on the other hand, makes itself immune to the demand for revision.

People of faith, conflict complains, keep on trusting in God no matter how little evidence there is to support this trust. Regardless of how chaotic and troubled the world is and how much suffering and death occur, the faithful still cling to their God. In the face of enormous suffering and evil, instead of renouncing their faith in God as reasonable people should, Jews recite the words of Job (13:15): "See, he will kill me: I have no hope; but I will defend my ways to his face." After Jesus's execution, his followers ended up trusting in God even more than before. Today, Muslims all over the world trust unconditionally in Allah no matter how many setbacks and horrors they suffer. To this intransigence, conflict responds, If there is nothing that can conceivably invalidate your faith, then looking for evidence to support it is completely irrelevant. How utterly opposed faith is to the spirit of science!

The conflict position holds that that faith is unreasonable because it can provide no evidence of God, scientific or otherwise. In this book conflict is exemplified by "scientific skepticism," the belief that science contradicts faith. Scientific skeptics, such as the New Atheists, are people who insist that faith in God has no basis in observable reality. Faith, they claim, is rooted in fantasy, whereas science is based on observable, empirically available data. Faith is highly emotional and subjective, whereas science is dispassionate, impersonal, and objective. Consequently there must exist an insuperable mutual hostility between science and faith.

The remaining chapters of this book examine numerous expressions of the conflict approach. However, scientific skeptics are not alone in insisting that faith clashes with science. Many devout religious believers also think science, at least at times, contradicts their beliefs. They are opposed, especially, to the Darwinian theory of evolution. About half of the Christians in the United States, for example, maintain that "secular science" like that of Darwin should be rejected whenever it seems to contradict the letter of scripture. Christian opponents of evolution are known as "creationists." If you ever visit the new Creation Museum in Kentucky you will notice that each display highlights the opposition between what the exhibits label "biblical science" on the one hand and "secular science," especially evolutionary biology, on the other. For creationists, Darwin is wrong and the Bible is right. Chapter 3 considers the topic of evolution and faith in much more detail. For now it is enough to observe the strong sense of opposition to evolutionary science that exists in large sectors of the religious community.

Nevertheless, in this book conflict refers not to religious opposition to science but to the claims of the "scientific skeptics." These are scientists and scientifically educated people who believe that science is the *only* reliable road to truth—a belief known as "scientism"—and that the natural world available to science is literally all there is. This belief is often referred to as "scientific naturalism" and sometimes as "scientific materialism." Scientism and scientific naturalism are the main components of what this book calls "conflict."

Conflict rules out the existence of God because it finds no scientific evidence for the existence of anything beyond the natural world. Many atheists, of course, reject the idea of God for reasons other than its apparent incompatibility with science. To some, the idea of God seems morally and emotionally repugnant. However, intellectually speaking, the foundation of most serious contemporary atheism is an amalgam of scientism and scientific naturalism. Today many academics and journalists are committed to the conflict position. They assume, often without argument, that science cannot be reconciled with faith and theology. (By theology, once again, this book means the large body of reflection and speculation on the meaning of faith in God by Jewish, Christian, and Muslim thinkers.)

CONTRAST

Other highly educated people, including scientists and theologians, see no contradiction whatsoever between faith and science. Each, they maintain, is valid within its own clearly defined sphere of interest. Hence neither can be judged by the cognitive standards of the other. In other words, there is contrast but not opposition between the two. Science and faith have completely different interests and employ distinct methods of inquiry. So it makes no sense to place one in competition with the other.

Why then do so many people today still have the impression that faith and theology are irreconcilable with science? According to contrast, it is because they are confused about the respective roles of each. This confusion has been around since the beginning of the scientific revolution in the sixteenth and seventeenth centuries. In the early modern period, the word science was not yet in use, and even today philosophers are still trying to clarify the meaning of scientific method. In any case, the church's failure to distinguish carefully between theological beliefs and the experimental methods of science led to the unfortunate condemnation of Galileo by ecclesiastical officials in 1633. Confusion still exists today when people of faith express distrust of modern science and when scientific skeptics assume that theology is an obsolete form of science that must now be thrown out. Those who approach this discussion from the contrast perspective claim that the New Atheists, especially Richard Dawkins, mistakenly assume that the idea of God is a scientific hypothesis and as a result wrongly conclude that only modern scientific method can decide whether or not God exists.[2] In fact, according to the contrast view, the awareness of God comes to people of faith through a completely different kind of experience from that of sensation or scientific observation.

To avoid conflict, therefore, contrast requires that both scientists and people of faith stick to their own turf. The fundamental principle of contrast is simple: *Keep faith and science separate!* To compare or oppose them to each other leads only to needless complication.[3] Distinct sets of claims can be opposed to each other, after all, only if they are competing for the same goal. To contrast, however, science and theology are playing different "games" by respectively different sets of rules. So it makes no sense to place them in competition with or opposition to each other. Science is concerned with the physical *causes* of events in the natural world. Theology asks about the ultimate *meaning* of the world and human existence. Science solves physical problems, whereas theology points toward the divine mystery that encompasses and gives existence and purpose to the world. Science asks *how* things came to be and how they work; theology asks *why* the world exists at all and whether it has a kind of importance that science cannot comprehend.

By sharply segregating science from faith and theology, therefore, contrast seeks to avoid the confusion that leads to conflict. It respects both science and theology as independent modes of inquiry. Theology is not cut out to do science, and science cannot settle the question of God's existence or the nature of ultimate reality. Why not? Simply because scientific method by definition leaves out all questions about meaning, purpose, values, and God. Science strictly speaking is not "wired" to provide commentary on the ultimate origin, destiny, or meaning of things. Whenever scientists hold forth on such issues—as they often do—contrast points out that they are doing so not as scientists but as philosophers and even propagandists.

Among the latter, according to the defenders of contrast, are scientific skeptics who, like the rest of us, usually carry with them belief systems or worldviews of their own, even though they seldom admit it. Their belief system is not theism, but scientism. Scientism, contrast emphasizes, is not the same thing as science. Science is a fruitful method of learning some important things about the physical world, but there are other ways of knowing as well. Contrast is completely open to science, but it rejects scientism's confusion of science with the unscientific *belief* that science is the only reliable way to find truth.

Contrast points out that devotees of scientism not only place absolute trust in scientific method but that they also seek to gain followers through their own version of missionary activity. Today this solicitation flourishes in college and university classrooms as well as in high-profile journals and Internet blogs. Contrast finds the most unembarrassed flaunting of scientism in the writings of the New Atheists whom you will meet occasionally in these pages. The New Atheists, however, are not alone. Many educated people trust in science almost as though, like the gods of religions, it will bring salvation in the form of deliverance from the original sin of prescientific ignorance.

Contrast claims that the proponents of scientism contradict themselves. Followers of scientism are unable to demonstrate by way of scientific experimentation the truth of their own fundamental assumption that science is the only reliable road to truth. Devotees of scientism *believe* unconditionally and passionately in the power of science to clear up all confusion about the world. Yet they cannot justify this belief scientifically. Scientism tells us to take nothing on faith, and yet it takes faith to make a commitment to scientism. Clearly then, scientism is logically self-contradictory. Reasonable people, contrast maintains, are obliged by logic to reject it.

Contrast, therefore, forcefully reminds readers that it is not science, but scientism, that conflicts with faith and theology. Contrast persistently advises us that it is not science, but scientism, that has emptied modern culture of its religious depth. Science is not to blame. So contrast cautions us to be alert to the ways in which the conflict approach—embraced by contemporary scientific skeptics— labels as "science" what is really a mixture of science, scientism, and scientific naturalism.

Contrast views the marriage of science with scientism as a misbegotten union that can at times unfortunately turn people of faith against science altogether. This is a point of interest for anyone interested in science education, which most informed people now agree is generally quite poor, especially in the United States. From contrast's point of view, the New Atheists and many other scientific skeptics ironically promote scientific ignorance by arbitrarily declaring that science goes best with atheism. Since 80 to 90 percent of U.S. citizens believe in God, such a message is hardly likely to muster much support. Contrast emphasizes, therefore, that science is neutral on the question of God. Science simply does not ask about God, ultimate meaning, or moral values. Therefore, it has nothing to say about them. Contrast's persistent plea: Keep science and faith separate!

CONVERGENCE

Our third approach, convergence, maintains that contrast may be an important first step toward clarity, but it still fails to satisfy those who seek a more coherent picture of reality. The human urge to unify knowledge is too powerful to suppress indefinitely. Contrast, therefore, may help us think lucidly about both science and faith, but it leads our conversation to a frustrating standoff.[4] Doesn't the new cosmic story of a 13.7 billion-year-old universe have theological consequences? Don't the breakthrough ideas of Charles Darwin, Albert Einstein, Georges Lemaître, Edwin Hubble, Stephen Hawking, Francis Crick, and other scientific discoverers have any relevance to faith and theology?

Convergence insists that they do. It refuses to leave the world divided indefinitely into separate spheres of inquiry as defined by contrast. It agrees with contrast that science and faith are each concerned with different kinds of questions. However, convergence claims that theology and scientific knowledge cannot be walled up in completely separate compartments of the human mind and culture indefinitely. New discoveries in cosmology, geology, biology, and neuroscience do have implications for faith and theology. A mature faith, according to convergence, is willing to make adjustments, and theology must change and grow as new discoveries reshape our understanding of nature. History shows that theologies have often, if not always, undergone wholesome transformation in the wake of new scientific understanding.

Convergence looks for an open-ended conversation between scientists and theologians. The word convergence as used here implies that a fully satisfactory synthesis of science and theology has not yet occurred. The ongoing conversation between science and theology is never fully finished. Convergence seeks to avoid a facile marriage of the two, but it allows for interaction and dialogue between them. It forbids both conflation and mutual isolation. Convergence insists on preserving the differences between science and faith, but it also seeks to clarify their relationship. It proposes that scientific understanding of the world can broaden the horizon of one's religious faith, and that the perspective of faith can deepen one's understanding of the meaning of scientific discoveries.

Convergence, therefore, is especially interested in exploring the theological significance of what this book is calling the "new cosmic story" outlined briefly in the introduction. Convergence doesn't try to prove God's existence from science, but it does look for deeper meaning in our still fresh scientific realization that life evolves and the universe is still coming into being. Convergence does not attempt to shore up faith's claims by appealing to specific patches of scientific evidence. However, it cannot help asking what the new cosmic story might *mean* for people of faith.

The theistic faith traditions characteristically strive to instill in their followers a special way of looking at the world. Rooted in the story of Abraham, who was called into a new future by a promising God, the prophetic faith traditions (Judaism, Christianity, and Islam) all forbid despair and cosmic pessimism. They think of genuine faith as accompanied by hope, a confidence that undreamed-of possibilities are latent even in the most desperate of situations. In the age of science, authentic faith is a steadfast conviction that the future is open and that an incalculable fulfillment awaits not only human beings but also the entire cosmos.

Does such a hopeful point of view contradict science? Not according to convergence. At first sight, faith's hopeful state of mind may seem incompatible with the "realism" of science. However, as the reader will discover, the convergence approach in each of the following chapters argues that there is a remarkable accord between a faith perspective shaped by a sense of reality's promise and the character of the universe as depicted by contemporary cosmology. The entire long quest by science for increasing coherence and intelligibility is completely consistent with the theme of hope that underlies Abrahamic theology. This, at least, is how convergence sees it.

Perhaps the most prominent exemplar of convergence is the renowned paleontologist and Jesuit priest, Pierre Teilhard de Chardin (1881–1955). Teilhard, writing in the early to mid-twentieth century, was one of the first scientists to observe that evolutionary biology, geology, and cosmology together provide an exciting new picture of a still emerging universe, and that this picture can enrich and renew religious faith. He was among the first scientists to realize that the whole universe is a *story* rather than a fixed state. At the same time, he argued that a mature faith and theology can open our minds to levels of meaning in the cosmic story that conventional science cannot reach.

Theology, convergence points out, can provide no scientific information, nor can science generate theological systems. Taken together, however, science and theology can contribute to a fresh, intellectually plausible and morally exciting vision of what's going on in the universe. Teilhard did not look to science to validate his religious beliefs, nor did he conflate science with faith. He thought, however, that faith and theology need to take seriously what science is now telling us about the universe we live in. Science, he argued, can deepen our understanding of God, just as an appropriate understanding of God can add a dimension of depth and meaning to the discoveries of science.[5] Teilhard, therefore, provides much of the inspiration for the convergence position as it responds to each of this book's topics.

Finally, convergence argues not only that scientific discoveries raise important issues for faith and theological inquiry but also that central theological teachings are inherently supportive of scientific inquiry. Faith and scripture have no special insights to dish out about the physical characteristics of the universe. Faith's inherent support for science in no way involves the endorsement of any particular scientific hypothesis or theory. Rather, faith's support of science goes much deeper: faith and theology can justify a scientist's spontaneous belief that the universe is *intelligible*.

How so? At the roots of any good scientist's restless desire to make sense of things lies an undeniable confidence that the world makes sense and that truth is always worth seeking. Faith and theology, according to convergence, add support to the entire scientific enterprise by preparing our minds for the adventure of scientific discovery and truth seeking. They can shore up the fundamental trust that is needed to undertake scientific inquiry. Einstein himself acknowledged that science has to reach outside of itself to find the motivation to pursue the truth consistently. Science is dependent, he said, on a kind of religious faith:

> Science can only be created by those who are thoroughly imbued with the aspiration toward truth and understanding. This source of feeling, however, springs from the sphere of religion. To this there also belongs the faith in the possibility that the regulations valid for the world of existence are rational, that is, comprehensible to reason. I cannot conceive of a genuine scientist without that profound faith.[6]

Convergence does not claim that a scientist has to believe in God to be a good scientist. It affirms only that faith in God is supportive of, and provides the deepest and most reasonable justification of, the *trust* that a scientific mind needs if it is to persist in the often difficult struggle for understanding and truth. Whether the scientist believes in God or not, scientific inquiry requires of the scientist a robust faith that nature is lawful, predictable, and intelligible. Even a scientific skeptic, as Einstein illustrates, has to trust that nature, though often surprising, is never capricious. Doing science requires a confident expectation that the scientific search can lead to deeper understanding down the road. This confidence is essential to both launching and sticking with the scientific adventure. In its belief that nature's coherence is ultimately grounded in an infinite divine wisdom, meaning, and truth, theology provides an entirely reasonable foundation for the trust needed by every good scientist.

In summary, then, convergence makes two main points. First, scientific discoveries can expand and enrich our sense of God. And second, faith's sense of an inexhaustible meaning and truth underlying the universe provides a soft breeze that bears the sails of a scientific mind ever onward toward further discoveries. A good scientist, in other words, can easily be a devout person of faith. Convergence acknowledges that our minds are never large enough to take in the whole horizon of being at any given moment. Yet it holds that faith can stir the scientist to press onward—beyond the narrowness of current understanding—in search of ever more breadth and depth. Faith and theology can quietly energize the enterprise of scientific discovery. Scientists can be people of faith, in other words, because their various disciplines thrive on the conviction that the world they are exploring does make sense. Abandoning oneself to such trust does not lead one into conflict with science, according to convergence, but instead prepares a human mind for the great journey of scientific discovery.

CHAPTER 2

Does Science Rule Out a Personal God?

Under each of the three subtitles of each chapter you will find a different answer to that chapter's question. As outlined in chapter 1, these approaches are called "conflict," "contrast," and "convergence." To dramatize their distinctiveness, allow imaginary spokespersons for each perspective to address you in a blunt and provocative way. Not every idea relevant to each approach can be expressed in a single chapter, but by the end of the book you should have a more rounded picture of each of the three points of view. As you read each chapter, figuratively place large quotation marks around each of the three positions, and be sure to place yourself in the conversation as well.

CONFLICT

Our answer to this chapter's question is an emphatic "yes."[1] Science rules out the existence of a personal God. How can any scientifically educated person still believe in the God of Judaism, Christianity, and Islam? Science offers no evidence that a caring, responsive God exists.[2] In fact, science suggests just the opposite: at bottom the universe is blind, mindless, and impersonal. Here is a sketch of our conflict position:[3]

1. Apart from nature, which includes human beings and their cultural creations such as language and art, there is nothing. There is no evidence of the existence of God, the soul,

or life beyond death. Nature is all there is, and science is the most reliable way to understand it.

2. Since no personal God exists, the natural world must be self-originating. It has no explanation beyond itself. The universe "simply is."

3. The universe has no purpose. Science has found no evidence that anything of lasting importance is going on in the universe. The cosmos is a long story, but the story has no point. Everything, including all human achievements, will perish in a final cosmic deep freeze, as most cosmologists now agree. So you have no good reason to believe in a personal God who gives permanent significance to your life or to the cosmos. Nevertheless, you can create a meaning for your own life all by yourself. We expand on this point in chapter 11.

4. Since God doesn't exist, everything that happens in the world, including your intellectual and moral activities, and even your religious longings if you have any, is purely natural and can be fully explained by science.

5. Good behavior does not require belief in a God who decides what is right and wrong or who rewards and punishes. People can figure out for themselves what is good and bad. Science now explains how we can be good without God (see chapter 8).

Before the age of science, we concede, it was easier for people to believe in God than it is today. It is not surprising that scientifically ignorant people still explain events in nature by attributing them to the whims of deities or to a personal God. The good things that happen to people seem to be gifts of a beneficent deity, and the bad things — storms, floods, earthquakes, tsunamis, droughts, plagues, and famines — make sense as divine punishment for sin.

Science, however, has desacralized the world and chased the gods away for good. After examining natural occurrences scientifically, we have found that only mindless matter lurks beneath the surface. Everything is reducible to atomic units and physical processes. The deeper science digs, the more impersonal the universe appears. As the atheist physicist Steven Weinberg correctly points out, the universe bears no imprint of an "interested" God.[4] Admittedly, the laws of nature as understood by an earlier physics may at one time have suggested the existence of a distant divine lawgiver. But since the time of Newton (1642–1727), science has increasingly demonstrated that whatever happens in the world can be accounted for by the blind laws of chemistry and physics. The world-famous cosmologist Stephen Hawking has rightly argued recently that the impersonal laws of nature are even sufficient to explain how the universe got here in the first place. Big Bang cosmology has now made the idea of a creator unnecessary.[5] After taking into account contemporary physics and cosmology, it seems silly to look for an infinite divine love, a kindly face, or an eternal providential care behind the patently mindless workings of nature.

Not only physics but also biology supports our naturalistic exclusion of a personal God. It is true that as late as the early twentieth century some religious scientists, nostalgic for mysticism, conjectured that the emergence of living organisms from dead matter was a miraculous occurrence. Only a living God, they assumed, could have breathed life into the cosmos. By the beginning of the twenty-first century, however, biochemistry and molecular biology had demonstrated that the secret of life lies in the interaction of large molecules known as amino and nucleic acids. Vitalism, the belief that a nonmaterial force brings life into the universe, is now obsolete. There is nothing miraculous or extraordinary about life at all. The specific features of living organisms, including human beings, can now be fully accounted for by what evolutionary biology calls "natural selection." We comment in more detail on the atheistic implications of evolution in chapter 3.

You might object, as many scientifically uninformed religious believers do, that the complexity of life is so staggering that it requires an intelligent designer. And you might suppose that the existence of human consciousness is so wondrously improbable that only an intelligent God could have brought it about. Yet the biological and cognitive sciences, including neuroscience, evolutionary psychology, and the study of artificial intelligence, have now advanced to the point at which we can predict that human consciousness—including what you call "personality"—will eventually be accounted for by scientific method alone.

You may still be unconvinced that your own mind could have come into existence without the influence of a divine intelligence. You might side with the psalmist who asks, "He who planted the ear, does he not hear? He who formed the eye, does he not see?" (Ps 94:9–10). So also, you may wonder, doesn't it take a divine personal intelligence to make human intelligence?

Not at all. Science gives us a purely natural explanation for the existence and operations of your mind. In his erudite book *Consciousness Explained*, the philosopher Daniel Dennett, one of the most celebrated contemporary defenders of conflict, argues convincingly that your consciousness is no more mysterious, and no less physical, than any other physical process.[6] Beneath your own personality lies an impersonal universe. Your body secretes consciousness through your brain and nervous system in essentially the same way that your stomach digests food.

Obviously science has not yet explained consciousness in complete detail, but we believe it will do so eventually. Science takes time, and sooner or later it will demolish the antiquated notion that your mind is somehow distinct from your brain, or that you have an immortal soul or self (see chapter 7). Then it will become clear that the existence of a personal God is not needed to make sense of your own intelligence and personality. These have emerged by way of evolutionary processes over millions of years in an essentially mindless universe. Your ancestors, ignorant of science, simply projected their own personalities onto the impersonal universe, and this wishful thinking is what originally led to the idea of a personal God. Science now makes it imperative to discard this childish idea once and for all.

The most celebrated scientist of the twentieth century, Albert Einstein, supports our objection to the idea of a personal God. It is true that Einstein sometimes talked about "God," and he even spoke publicly of himself as a religious man.[7] He was religious, however, only in the sense that he felt there was something permanently mysterious about the universe and that there exists a domain of permanent values to which the scientist must be devoutly committed. However, he forcefully rejected belief in the personal, responsive God of Jews, Christians, and Muslims. He thought that the idea of a God who could answer prayers was the product of primitive superstition. Such a belief, he claimed, is the main cause of conflicts between science and religion. When he said, "God does not play at dice with the universe," he meant simply that the universe runs by inviolable, impersonal physical laws. His occasional use of the word God has misled some readers to think of Einstein as a theist of a sort, but he used theological language only to stress his belief that the universe is lawful, eternal, and intelligible. Like his intellectual mentor, the philosopher Baruch Spinoza (1632–77), he was convinced that nature is all that exists. We who follow the conflict approach fully agree.

CONTRAST

Once again, picture here a committee of spokespersons representing the second of our three points of view and speaking directly—and forcefully—to you.

In line with the distinctions made in this book's first chapter, those of us who embrace the contrast position have a big question for the scientific skeptics to whom you have just been listening: Is it really science that rules out the existence of a personal God? Or isn't it instead scientism and its offspring scientific naturalism? Isn't it these beliefs, and not science, that contradict theology?

Recall here that this book defines *scientism* as the belief that science is the only reliable road to truth. And it defines *scientific naturalism* as the belief that only the natural world available to scientific understanding really exists. Scientism and scientific naturalism, we emphasize throughout, are not science but instead unwarranted assumptions about science. In our view there is contrast, but no conflict, between science and faith. The relevant conflict is between two belief systems: theistic faith on the one hand and scientism (which leads to scientific naturalism) on the other.

So our question to Weinberg and Hawking, as well as to Einstein, is this: Does your expertise in physics or cosmology qualify you to decide whether faith in a personal God is reasonable or not? Followers of contrast ask this question because, as the previous chapter pointed out, all the natural sciences by definition leave out consideration of anything that has to do with God. No wonder science can't find God! Scientific method isn't able to pick up any signals of a deity even if God exists. Genuine science is content to express its understanding of the universe in abstract models and mathematical equations. Science as such confines itself to an impersonal, dispassionate description of the natural world. Physical science would be completely crippled if it got involved in pursuing questions such as whether a personal God exists.

The existence of a personal God, therefore, is simply not an issue that physics, or for that matter any other natural science, can settle by itself. Hence, we insist that the alleged impersonality of the universe alluded to by Hawking, Weinberg, and Einstein is not a discovery of science but an invention of scientism. In our opinion, moreover, devotees of scientism are just as religious as our prescientific ancestors were. Scientism and scientific naturalism provide answers to ageless religious questions: Where do we come from? What is our true identity? Is there anything permanent and imperishable? What is the final destiny of everything?

These are not scientific but religious questions. Even though the answers that scientism and scientific naturalism give are dispiriting, they function nevertheless as a belief system or worldview that goes far beyond what science itself can tell us. Scientific naturalism addresses humanity's persistent religious questions, but it does so by first reducing everything that exists to physical or material stuff. This approach is sometimes called "reductionism," and it leads to a naturalistic worldview often referred to as "materialism" or "physicalism." We suggest that the clarity and measurability, along with the seemingly hard-rock realness of material stuff, appeals to a deeply mystical longing to merge one's mind and life with some underlying unity—in this case mindless matter.

Materialism, the belief that only matter is real, satisfies therefore not only the mind's desire to simplify things but also the human longing for a solid and durable ground upon which to rest our anxious and perishable lives. Furthermore, the materialist dream of exhaustive physical explanation functions as the holy grail of scientism's version of the long human quest for complete enlightenment. The hope for full revelation through science gives scientific materialists a reason for getting up in the morning. It is this set of beliefs, not science, that contradicts faith's trust in a personal God.

In today's academic world, scientism has become so deeply entangled with well-established scientific ideas that it is often difficult to unravel them. The work of the outspoken atheist evolutionist Richard Dawkins offers an especially clear example of this confusion.[8] "It may be," he says, "that humanity will never reach the quietus of complete understanding, but if we do, I venture the confident prediction that it will be science, not religion, that brings us there. And if that sounds like scientism, so much the better for scientism."[9] Dawkins is by no means alone in his religiously devout commitment to scientism. Alex Rosenberg, the chair of Duke University's philosophy department, expresses the creed of many contemporary philosophers, scientists, and journalists when he explicitly endorses scientism as "the philosophical theory that treats science as our most reliable source of knowledge and scientific method as the most effective route to knowledge."[10]

Scientism, even though there is no scientific basis for it, is quite influential in academic and intellectual circles. Contrast, however, has much more respect for the integrity of science than do the disciples of scientism. We carefully distinguish science not only from theistic faith but also from *all* belief systems, including scientism and materialism. The naïve merging of science with scientism exemplified by Dawkins and Rosenberg has led countless modern intellectuals to the quite unscientific claim that science is irreconcilable with theology. Contrast, however, holds that there is no contradiction between pure science and genuine theology. Neither scientific method nor scientific discovery contradicts the idea of a personal God.

When those of us who espouse contrast talk about a personal God, after all, we are not referring to illusory ideas roaming aimlessly about in human imaginations. We are talking about powerful *experi-*

ences analogous to, and no less real than, what happens in the encounter of one human person with another. We are referring to the experience of a divine "Thou" that has addressed us, grasped hold of us, and challenged us to a personal transformation deeper than any other experience we have ever had. The experience of God comes to us not through impersonal scientific method, but through a distinctly *interpersonal* mode of awareness.

Devotees of scientism, of course, complain that we should not believe anything without sufficient scientific evidence. However, our reply to this objection is twofold. First, as we have already pointed out, there is no scientific evidence for scientism either. Scientism itself is a belief that has nothing to do with science except to exaggerate the power and scope of scientific inquiry. But second, and more important, who's to say that no evidence underlies our trust in a personal God?

In fact, there are two main kinds of evidence. The first we may refer to as "spectator evidence." This is the kind of evidence we gather by means of sense experience or through instruments of observation such as microscopes and telescopes. It is this sort of evidence that science seeks.[11]

However, there is also "transformative evidence." You meet with this kind of evidence every day in your encounter with other persons. You have experienced intimate interpersonal connections with friends and others who have loved you, challenged you, and changed you, often dramatically. But you can experience transformative evidence only by making yourself vulnerable to the inner life — or subjectivity — of other persons. When contrast talks about the experience of a personal God, therefore, we mean something analogous to what happens when you allow yourself to be loved by another personal subject. This is the kind of evidence that radically alters your life in the very process of your experiencing it. Our point then is that faith in a personal God is based upon transformative evidence, not purely scientific or spectator evidence.

The transformative experience that we associate with faith in a personal God sometimes takes place in the privacy of our individual lives, but it also occurs in the context of a community and tradition associated with a particular set of religious images, rituals, and stories. Of this we are assured in a way that completely eludes the search for the kind of spectator evidence that underlies scientific ideas. In any case, we do not need the support of impersonal, objectifying science to corroborate our sense of being addressed by a personal God. The experience of faith occurs quite apart from anything that science can illuminate by itself.

It is sadly ludicrous, therefore, when those who embrace the con-flict position—skeptics such as Dawkins and the other New Atheists—demand that we give them *scientific* evidence for our faith. Such a requirement is comparable to asking for scientific proof that someone has fallen in love with you. We did not wish for an encounter with God. More often than not we have tried to run away from it, anxious that it might challenge us to live our lives in a deeper way. The per-sonal transformation required by faith is not easy or cheap. Many of us struggle at times to avoid the demands of faith. We may even find excuses for this avoidance by taking refuge in a scientism that encour-ages us to interpret faith as nothing more than wishful thinking. Still, many of us have discovered to our joy that the transformation faith brings is deeply liberating, expanding, and fulfilling. By risking this experience we have found our faith to be truthful in the deepest pos-sible sense.

Following the wisdom of our faith traditions, we believe that the "faculty" through which we become aware of a divine subject needs to be awakened in us. This doesn't happen simply by throwing a switch. For it is essential to faith that we frankly confess our own powerlessness to accomplish this awakening. What makes faith so fragile among the educated these days is that the human capacity to experience faith's transformative invitation has gone into a deep slumber. Sometimes it is coated over by pessimistic cosmological assumptions allegedly based on science (see chapter 11). Nevertheless, even though the capacity for faith has atrophied in a culture of scientism and scientific naturalism, we believe that it can still be stirred to life once we realize how limited science is in excavating the depths of reality.

CONVERGENCE

Once again, imagine here a group of spokespersons addressing you from yet another perspective on the relationship between science and faith.

The contrast position just summarized has the merit of distinguishing clearly between science and faith as well as between science and scientism. However, the contrast approach overlooks opportunities for a more open and genuine dialogue between science and faith. It is good to make distinctions, but it is important to clarify connections as well. Convergence emphasizes that scientific findings often have implications for how people of faith think about God. Scientific *method* by itself says nothing about a personal God, of course, and theology can provide no scientific information. However, scientific *discoveries* do make a difference in how we think about God. This is especially true of science's recent discovery that the cosmos is an immensely long and still unfolding story.

Discoveries by physics, astrophysics, and biology, in other words, do raise interesting questions about whether the idea of a personal God is believable today. The question of a personal God arises most pointedly when we ponder the theological implications of evolutionary biology. We look at the question of theology and evolution more closely in chapter 3, so here we shall be content simply to address the suspicion many educated people have today that astrophysics and cosmology now rule out the whole notion of a personal God.

When we say that God is "personal" we mean that God is "interested" in what goes on in the world, including our own individual lives. To call God personal means that the creator of the universe is endowed with boundless intelligence, freedom, love, fidelity, and responsiveness. "Personal God" means a lot of other things besides, but at the very least it means that God must have the capacity to form deep relationships, to care, to love, to make and keep promises. A personal God, if God exists, would have to embody these qualities to an eminent degree or in a maximal way.

After Galileo, Newton, Darwin, Einstein, Hubble, and Hawking, however, hasn't the cozy prescientific universe that for centuries harbored our thoughts about a personal God now faded away? Traditionalist believers in God are bewildered theologically by the new story of the universe that scientific explorers have uncovered. To avoid dealing with it, some of them fall back on the contrast approach. Others, especially those who take their holy books literally, reject new cosmological and biological discoveries altogether. Meanwhile, theologically uninformed scientific naturalists such as the New Atheists join with their creationist adversaries in taking sacred scriptures literally also. Their own biblical literalism leads the New Atheists to mock ancient scriptures as useless because the holy books fail to give them a quality grade of modern scientific information. The Bible, they assume anachronistically, should be ignored as an obsolete display of human ignorance because, as Sam Harris declares, it has nothing to say "about electricity or about DNA, or about the actual age and size of the universe."[12]

Convergence, however, rejects such astounding displays of literalism and looks for a much more nuanced way of relating scientific discoveries to faith and theology. Consider, for example, the nearly 14 billion years the universe has taken to bring human beings into existence. Scientific naturalists and biblical literalists consider this to be a colossal waste of time. Deep time makes the notion of a caring personal deity who somehow oversees the cosmic process quite unbelievable. Why would a personal God, if God exists, allow the universe to get so old before producing human persons? And why is the universe so spatially expansive? Isn't our own existence as personal beings simply an accidental afterthought in a vastly impersonal cosmic production? Doesn't nature itself contradict the idea of a "personal" God?

This is not an entirely new question. Pessimistic ancient philosophers felt the universe to be essentially impersonal, governed by fate or capricious deities with no sense of fairness and justice. Some Eastern traditions still suppose that the impersonal law of karma — that you reap what you sow — rules over everything. Today many if not most prominent intellectuals think of the cosmos as essentially mindless, lifeless, and purposeless. In the seventeenth century the pessimistic philosopher Blaise Pascal (1623–62), though a believer in

31

God, had difficulty connecting the God of Abraham and Jesus to the immensity of time and space, a vastness that science was just beginning to uncover. Were Pascal here today he would probably endorse contrast, and he would be more religiously anxious than ever. As our scientific understanding of the cosmos increases, so also does our impression of the silence of the heavens. It isn't hard for many people these days to believe that the universe is impersonal through and through.

Nevertheless, instead of running away from science's new sense of the universe's spatial and temporal enormity, convergence takes this great discovery as an invitation to enlarge significantly the picture of the infinitely generous and promising God that our faith traditions have handed on to us. We agree that our theology needs to outgrow the one-planet deity of prescientific religious understanding. This adjustment, however, in no way contradicts our classical creeds. Instead it is faithful to the traditional theological axiom that our sense of God must always remain infinitely larger than the universe. *Deus semper major*—God is always greater than anything we can conceive or imagine. No matter how vast the universe grows in the eyes of science, then, it is always surpassed by the limitlessness that faith attributes to God. Convergence sees the new growth in scientific understanding of the universe as an invitation to amplify rather than abandon our sense of the greatness and generosity of God.

How, though, can we think of the infinite God as personal? Can we still address God as "Thou" in a universe that seems so immense and impersonal to many scientifically educated people? If there exists a personal God, this God would have to be "interested," not only in persons but also in the *whole* cosmos that science has revealed to us. Moreover, the Abrahamic traditions see divine personality especially epitomized in God's making and keeping of promises. So how might we connect nature, as science now understands it, to the idea of a personal, promising God?

One key to such a connection lies in the fact that the universe now shows itself to be a still unfinished drama of person-making. Each person sums up the creative cosmic process in a unique and irreplaceable way. The cosmic story has produced other kinds of being as well, of course, but our point is that the universe has never been essentially impersonal in the way that conflict's scientism narrowly decrees. The cosmic drama has held the promise of becoming personal ever since its beginning, and it still holds out the promise of even more unpredictable creative outcomes in the future. Even the earliest chapters of the story now appear in retrospect to have been configured in such a way as to favor the coming of life, subjectivity, striving, intelligence, freedom, and personality. Ours has never been an impersonal universe, so there is no basis in science for assuming that its ultimate source and foundation is impersonal.

This book provides ample opportunity for conflict to articulate its objections to what we have just said. So the conversation of science and faith will continue. For now let us just be clear that, in our view, nature is not a meaningless collection of entities floating eternally and impersonally in space. It is an immense narrative that begs to be *read* at different levels, not only with the quantitative measurements of science but also with the dramatic concerns of faith. From the perspective of faith, the universe is a not yet fully realized promise of becoming *more*, a promise that can easily be aligned with Abrahamic expectation.[13]

If science has shown the cosmos to be an unfinished drama, theology reads the drama as a journey into a future continually made new by God. God's personal care for creation consists in part of offering the universe a future that mere mortals cannot begin to imagine but which in our freedom we may choose to accept or refuse. In a sense, for convergence, God *is* the world's future. What could be more indicative of personal care than to open up a new future for all of creation? It is hard for us to conceive of a more magnanimous display of personal interest in the world than to seed it, even in the midst of countless apparent dead ends, with the promise of becoming *more*.[14]

Convergence, furthermore, interprets science's bounteous disclosure of the world's temporal and spatial magnitude as anything but a display of impersonality. On the contrary, this temporal and spatial expansiveness is connected essentially, not accidentally, to the eventual emergence of persons in evolution. The cosmic pessimist tries to show how insignificant human persons are when situated against the background of an unimaginably enormous and temporally prolonged universe. Proponents of conflict make a big deal of how, ever since Copernicus, science's expanding sense of cosmic immensity has dethroned us and rendered human persons increasingly unimportant. Convergence, however, understands the universe's temporal and spatial vastness not as waste but as a dramatic prologue to and context for the emergence of living, feeling, and conscious personal beings whose most treasurable attributes include their own capacity to make and keep promises.

The emergence of personal existence in the universe, including especially the precious reality of freedom, can be cooked up in no less a crucible than our Big Bang universe. The details of this proposal await further development in subsequent chapters. New developments in physics and cosmology, we can only suggest here, provide theology with resources for fertile new reflection on God's relation to a universe whose immensity was perhaps unimaginable in ages past. Science's new sense of nature as a story or drama allows us to locate the universe in the presence of an "ever greater" God whose "personal" interest in the world consists of faithfully presenting it with possibilities for becoming new. The sobering prospect that our present life-bearing universe will come to an end—perhaps trillions of years from now—does nothing to discourage our faith in a God who always deals with dead ends by opening up a new future.

In summary, while conflict thinks of humans as personal beings lost in a spatially immense and impersonal universe, convergence reads the universe as an unfinished drama that has always had the promise of flowering into mind, freedom, and personality. In a sense, the making of "subjects" is a major part of what the "objective" universe is all about. We unfold this thought in much more detail, starting in the following chapter.

CHAPTER 3

Is Faith Compatible with Evolution?

CONFLICT

In 1859 Charles Darwin (1809–82) published *On the Origin of Species* introducing his famous theory of evolution. Biologists today marvel at how well the theory has held up during the past century and a half. From the perspective of conflict, however, Darwin's theory of evolution marks the decisive defeat of the idea of God. The whole thrust of modern science has been to undermine faith in God, of course, but with Darwin as our champion we are now engaged in the final battle against religious superstition. Evolution is now our chief weapon in science's war against faith and theology.[1]

Only a brief look at Darwin's great discovery will show why we believe evolution rules out the existence of God. In the *Origin* Darwin noted that all living species produce more offspring than ever reach maturity. Only a lucky few organisms can adapt to their environments and live long enough to leave offspring. The mechanism of *natural selection* allows only the fittest to survive. *Fitness* means simply that some individuals have a better chance of surviving and reproducing than the unfortunate many. Most organisms and species lose out in what Darwin called the "struggle for existence."

So how could anyone honestly believe that a good, loving, and intelligent personal deity is responsible for this hash? Surely a beneficent creator would not have been so uninterested in the value of individual organisms as to allow most of them to perish at the hands of impersonal selection. Darwin's picture of life seems so unfair to the weakest instances of life that it makes the idea of a just and merciful God incredible. Evolutionary science, we are convinced, is incompatible with faith in a personal, providential God.

Yet, in spite of the apparent wastefulness of the process, conflict observes that the long journey of evolution has produced—without the help of any creative divine intelligence—a staggering diversity of life and millions of interesting new species, including eventually our own. So we agree with Darwin that the evolutionary view of life has a kind of "grandeur" to it. Theology, on the other hand, adds nothing to this great adventure of life.

Allow us to state even more forcefully why we must embrace the conflict position after looking at the life process through Darwin's eyes. Darwin's recipe for evolutionary change, including the occasional emergence of new species in the long history of life, consists of three Godless ingredients. These are accidents, impersonal natural selection, and a colossally wasteful amount of time.

First, accidents. The high degree of chance or randomness involved in the emergence and evolution of life refutes the idea of a designing deity. The origin of life, chemically speaking, was purely random rather than intelligently planned. Furthermore, innumerable accidents in cosmic and geological history were required to fashion a planet hospitable to life. Our own existence depends as much on unplanned cosmic events as on nature's laws. For example, 65 million years ago an asteroid crashed into the Yucatán Peninsula, causing an abrupt cooling of the planet that wiped out the dinosaurs and other prehistoric animals. This astronomical accident, however, opened up new opportunities for mammals to thrive, so that eventually primates and humans were permitted to come onto the scene. So, if the existence of our own species depends on such mindless accidents as asteroid impacts in natural history, it baffles us that so many educated people still believe in an intelligent deity who watches over the world. Moreover, accident rather than intelligent design also underlies the variations—what today we would call "genetic mutations"—that provide the raw material for evolutionary change and diversity. How, therefore, can anyone reconcile the randomness in evolution with the idea of a divine intelligent designer?

Second, the ruthless working of natural selection is also incompatible with belief in divine providence. The idea of natural selection is Darwin's main contribution to science. Although other scientists before Darwin had suspected that life evolves over time, it was Darwin's great contribution to clarify the mechanism required for evolutionary change. Natural selection, as he called it, chooses for survival and reproduction only a small percentage of organisms, those that just happen to be adaptive. In view of natural selection's blind indifference and injustice, it should be clear that evolution poses problems for faith and theology. Darwin himself, we should note, became increasingly uncomfortable with the idea of a designing God and eventually lost his Christian faith.[2]

The third theologically disturbing aspect of Darwin's theory is the enormously wasteful amount of time it has taken for evolution to produce life and mind. Life, at least on Earth, did not begin until around 10 billion years after the Big Bang. Prior to the Cambrian Explosion more than 500 million years ago, life existed mostly as single cells. Our question then is why, if God exists, evolution has been so slow. If God is a creator, why is the divine production of life so much more inefficient than the projects of human engineers? Certainly if the universe were grounded in an intelligent deity, the emergence of living and thinking beings would not have taken so long or been so circuitous. The prodigious amount of time it has taken to produce these outcomes seems wasteful beyond anything human manufacturers or architects would ever put up with. Moreover, given all the time available, why would a creator fail to produce more perfectly designed and adaptive outcomes? Why are there so many "design flaws" in the organic world?[3]

A half-century or so before Darwin published the *Origin*, the Anglican cleric William Paley had argued that only an intelligent divine designer could account for the astonishing complexity of living organisms and their remarkable adaptation to specific environments. He compared the design of living organisms to the intricate interior mechanism of a watch. Then he concluded that just as the complex design of a watch requires an intelligent designer, so also does the even more complex makeup of living organisms. For Paley the intelligent designer, of course, is unmistakably the creator God of Abrahamic faith traditions.

As Richard Dawkins writes, however, Darwin instructs us that

> the only watchmaker in nature is the blind forces of physics, albeit deployed in a very special way. A true watchmaker has foresight: he designs his cogs and springs, and plans their interconnections, with a future purpose in the mind's eye. Natural selection, the blind, unconscious, automatic process which Darwin discovered, and which we now know is the explanation for the existence and apparent purposeful form of all life, has no purpose in mind. It has no mind and no mind's eye. It does not plan for the future. It has no vision, no foresight, no sight at all. If it can be said to play the role of watchmaker in nature, it is the *blind* watchmaker.[4]

Dawkins adds that after Darwin it has at last become possible for an informed person to be an "intellectually fulfilled atheist."[5] We fully agree with Dawkins and others who recognize that evolutionary biology is incompatible with what the book you are reading calls "faith."

CONTRAST

Even though representatives of the conflict position have tried to turn Darwin into a propagandist for atheism, he was really at most a reluctant agnostic. He did not cavalierly discard his religious heritage. While on his famous sea voyage he was still entertaining the prospect of becoming an Anglican clergyman. After he died he was buried in Westminster Abbey not far from Isaac Newton. He certainly did not disturb the religious establishment of his own day as much as the conflict position has maintained, nor should people of faith be disturbed by Darwin's ideas today.

Contrary to conflict, contrast maintains that Darwin's account of life is completely compatible with faith and theology. Contrast, you will recall, holds that science and faith are such different ways of looking at the world that they cannot meaningfully compete with each other. It is our view that Darwin's notion of natural selection is no more of a threat to faith than are the laws of physics and chemistry. The appearance of conflict arises not from evolutionary science but from a misguided confusion of evolutionary theory with scientism and scientific naturalism. This confusing synthesis may be called "evolutionary naturalism."

We are opposed not to evolution but to evolutionary naturalism. We also reject the anti-Darwinian pseudo-theological stances of creationism and intelligent design (ID). Creationists are biblical literalists who think the Bible teaches the "true" science. For them the biblical Book of Genesis functions not only as a religious tract but also as a source of reliable scientific information. If biblical accounts of life appear to contradict Darwin's evolutionary ideas, then creationists advise us to reject Darwin and take the biblical stories of life's creation as scientifically true.

Contrast, however, rejects biblical literalism because it could never have been the intention of ancient biblical authors to instruct their readers about contemporary science. We are befuddled, then, that not only creationists but also atheistic evolutionary naturalists read the Bible as though one of its functions is to provide scientific information. In the "Darwin wars" still going on today, one side (creationism) views the Book of Genesis as good science; the other (evolutionary naturalism) sees it as bad science. Both sides, however, mistakenly assume that the Bible should be a source of scientific information. In both cases it is a naïve biblical literalism that leads to their shared sense of contradiction between faith and science.[6]

Since the biblical writings were composed in a prescientific age, they should never be understood or evaluated in terms of modern scientific ways of understanding. Unfortunately, however, both creationists and evolutionary naturalists such as Dawkins, Dennett, and other disciples of the New Atheism impose anachronistic demands upon the

Bible, naïvely expecting it to be scientifically trustworthy. Contrast, on the other hand, always insists that the Bible's purpose is not to provide scientific information but instead to awaken believers to an infinite divine mystery that science cannot even begin to penetrate.

Recently, in public conversations about the merits of evolutionary biology, proponents of intelligent design have joined creationists in opposing Darwin's main ideas. Like creationists, ID proponents are generally conservative Christians, though not necessarily biblical literalists, who deny that natural causes alone can account for the astounding complexity of living organisms and subcellular mechanisms. Living complexity, according to ID, requires the special intervention of a supernatural cause. Most people, of course, associate this supernatural agency with the idea of God.[7]

Contrast agrees with scientists who point out that ID is a theological rather than scientific kind of explanation and that ID has no legitimate place in scientific research or public education. Contrast also holds that ID, like creationism, is objectionable both scientifically and theologically. First, the scientific evidence for evolution is undeniable. Geology, paleontology, radiometric dating, comparative anatomy, biogeography, embryology, genetics, and other fields of research provide sufficient evidence to make evolutionary theory one of science's greatest triumphs. Although evolutionary biology, like any other field of science, is always subject to improvement, contrast fully endorses scientific claims about the evidence for evolution as well as ongoing efforts to learn more about how evolution works.

Second, creationism and ID are not only scientifically but also *theologically* unacceptable. By placing the Book of Genesis in the same arena with science, as though the Bible could provide a competing "scientific" account of life, creationism turns our attention away from the deeper meaning of the biblical texts. And ID is theologically misguided when it tries to make room in science itself for what is patently a theological kind of explanation. Because most people associate ID with the creator God of biblical faith, it is theologically inappropriate to think of God as one cause among others in a chain of natural causes. So, to repeat, we reject creationism and ID for both scientific and theological reasons.

Contrast, however, acknowledges that the reaction to Darwin by both creationism and ID points to serious problems in the way some high-profile evolutionists present Darwin's ideas to students and the reading public. Richard Dawkins, Daniel Dennett, Jerry Coyne, E. O. Wilson, Stephen Jay Gould, and many other evolutionists spoil the credibility of Darwin's good science when they unwisely alloy evolutionary biology with a materialist worldview. Thus they distort the true nature of science by wrapping Darwin's discoveries snugly in the belief system we are calling "evolutionary naturalism." They contaminate Darwin's science by imposing on it an extraneous ideology. In doing so, they unnecessarily make Darwin's neutral scientific findings theologically unacceptable on any terms.

Evolutionary naturalists stubbornly claim that evolution is inherently opposed to faith in God. But in our opinion their uncritical fusion of Darwinian science with a materialist worldview is no less a violation of science than creationism and ID are. Dawkins, Coyne, and Dennett, for example, arbitrarily insist that accepting evolutionary biology requires that everybody also embrace materialist atheism. Yet this merger of science with atheism is no less contrary to the spirit of pure science than is the confusion of science with biblical creationism and ID.

In response to this confusion, contrast insists that science must be kept separate from all belief systems, whether theological or naturalistic. Confusing science with belief systems of any sort inevitably leads to the false impression of conflict between science and faith. By habitually adopting the contrast approach, however, you can always purify your scientific understanding from misrepresentation by ideologies or worldviews of all sorts. Scientists should stick to providing the evidence for evolution, and theologians should stick to their task of opening people up to the incomprehensible mystery of God that science can say nothing about. Evolution is not atheism but a purely scientific theory. What conflicts with faith in God is not evolutionary biology but evolutionary naturalism.

The reader may be wondering, nevertheless, how contrast reconciles the three theologically troubling ingredients of Darwin's recipe for life—namely, accidents, natural selection, and deep time—with the teachings of faith. Our response to this question is as follows.

First, the meaning of accident or chance is extremely hard to pin down. Our position is that "accident" is the name scientists give to any event that they have not yet been able to correlate with a more systematic understanding of nature. Certain events make no sense to us right now, but they may do so to God. Only God has the depth and breadth of perspective to grasp the full intelligibility of things. It is arrogant of mere mortals to demand final understanding of anything here and now. Our opponents in the conflict camp in effect play God by decreeing that evolutionary accidents are inherently unintelligible. How do they know this to be true? According to our contrast perspective, what people call "accidents" may make very good sense from a wider and deeper point of view than our limited senses and minds can ever command.

Conflict assumes omnisciently that if things don't make sense to science, they don't make sense at all. Contrast replies that there is no evidence to support the belief that science has an omniscient perspective on the universe. Indeed the evidence to the contrary is abundant from a cursory survey of the history of science itself, as most good scientists admit. Moreover, conflict's absolutist decree that evolution rules out God's existence violates the humility and reserve required for open-minded scientific inquiry. The contrast position is more modest. It trusts that the "randomness" of genetic mutations and asteroid impacts, for example, is an impression resulting from the narrowness of our human perspective on the universe. Faith confesses that any purely human angle of vision is always limited by our minds' inherent smallness. What appear now to be unintelligible accidents from the point of view of our impoverished human understanding are fully intelligible from the point of view of God's vision of the universe.

Second, complaints about the cruelty, struggle, and suffering that natural selection causes add absolutely nothing new to the problem of evil that people of faith have always had to face. Sincere believers in God are already familiar with the complaints of Job, the persecution of prophets, and the crucifixion of Jesus. They are fully aware of the history of violence and bloodshed endured by human beings and other forms of life throughout the ages. Contrast, therefore, has no more theological difficulty dealing with the alleged cruelty of natural selection than it does with the law of gravity or any other predictable routines of nature.

Even apart from biological evolution, we already know, for example, that gravity and the laws of thermodynamics care no more for individual lives or our inherent personal dignity than natural selection does. Gravity tugs indiscriminately on the good and the wicked or the weak and powerful alike, sometimes with deadly consequences. Very few people, however, have ever complained that gravity is an obstacle to faith in God. Contrast views natural selection no less leniently. Above all we try to remember that God's ways are not our ways. Our sense of the mystery of God is too profound to allow the limited perspective of science to undermine our faith. Indeed, the difficulties raised by science, and especially by Darwin, only challenge people of faith to trust all the more fervently in the unfathomable depths of God's wisdom and providence.

Third, the fact that evolutionary creativity takes an immense amount of time is not a problem at all for those who believe in the God of Abraham, Moses, Jesus, and Muhammad. The immensity of time as seen from our human experience is "like one day" in God's life. From the perspective of God's eternity, deep time is not the problem it is for us.

So, as you can see, contrast's response to evolutionary science is simply to trust in God in spite of all apparent incoherence. Faith, after all, has no real depth unless it is a leap into the unknown in the face of apparent absurdity. Faith is always trust "in spite of" difficulties that defy our finite capacity to understand. The Danish philosopher Søren Kierkegaard (1813–55), one of contrast's main sources of inspiration, has instructed us that the obsessive search for objective certainty deadens the very soul of faith. Genuine faith is possible only in the face of objective uncertainty. Evolution's severity is also consistent with the ancient religious notion that life is a "soul school" whose challenges purify us for the attainment of eternal life. If life posed no hardships, and if evolution were completely beneficent, would we ever have had the opportunity to develop our moral and spiritual character? No. Consequently, Darwin's ideas should cause no additional distress for people of faith.

CONVERGENCE

Contrast, as you have just seen, rightly exposes evolutionary naturalism as a mixture of science with materialist belief. Evolutionary naturalism is not science but instead a facile fusion of materialist atheism with science. It is this unnecessary mixture, not science as such, that leads many people mistakenly to think of Darwin as an enemy of faith. Contrast's sharp portrayal of the ideological biases in creationism and ID is a step in the right direction.

For many scientists and people of faith, however, contrast doesn't go far enough in the engagement of faith and theology with current biology. Convergence wants to take evolution more seriously than contrast does. Evolution is not just an innocuous scientific theory that theology can safely brush off. Darwin's science is an essential part of the new cosmic story that now provides the appropriate intellectual and spiritual framework for expressing faith's understanding of life, human existence, and God. To convergence, evolution turns out to be good for theology because it intensifies our sense that the universe is a drama to be read at different levels.

Unfortunately, devotees of contrast have not yet fully faced the fact that after Darwin our understanding of nature, life, humanity, and God cannot remain exactly the same as before. If theology is to make sense at all in today's intellectual climate, it requires fresh expression in evolutionary terms. Today we may even need to recast all of theology in terms of evolution. Darwin's seemingly dangerous ideas, along with those of Einstein and others, demand that we connect our theological reflections today to a narrative or dramatic understanding of nature. The real issue in this chapter, therefore, is not whether life's "designs" point to God or not. Both ID and evolutionary naturalism are too fixated on the question of whether life meets the criteria of good human engineering and architecture. Rather, for convergence the real issue after Darwin is whether the long drama of life that evolutionary science has uncovered is the carrier of a meaning that we can connect to our theological interests.

Evolutionary biology now allows us to think of life first of all as drama rather than design. How so? First, to have a drama there has to be some element of contingency, accident, or unpredictability. If a particular course of events were fully determined or predictable from the start, there would be no element of surprise or indeterminacy essential to the unfolding of a story. Second, however, a drama must have a thread of continuity that ties events and episodes together intelligibly, a coherence that can be clearly visible only in retrospect—that is, from the end of the story. Without some degree of consistency and predictability, the drama would dissolve into disconnected droplets. In that case it could carry no meaning. In the case of any narrative, however, its coherence, intelligibility, or meaning remains at least partly invisible while the story is still going on. As we shall remind you again and again, therefore, reading the story of life and the cosmos itself requires a posture of patience and silent waiting. Insisting on present certitude, along with an obsession with perfect design, destroys the possibility of discovering narrative coherence in the realm of life.

Third and finally, every drama or story requires a span of time long enough for events to unfold. Theologically, the question of the meaning of time, evolution, and the universe itself is inseparable from the ageless human employment of stories to make sense of any course of events, including the drama of life.

Notice, then, that Darwin's evolutionary recipe consists exactly of the three ingredients essential to any story: accidents plus the predictable working of natural selection plus a sufficiently long span of time. Darwin's portrayal of life is dramatic and therefore narrative to the core. Evolutionary biology has shown that life is not so much a set of architecturally interesting designs as it is a drama that begs to be read with a sense of expectation. Its meaning may eventually reveal itself, but perhaps only in the distant future.

That life is an ongoing story rather that a fixed or finalized arrangement of atoms, molecules, and cells is theologically significant. Stories are the medium through which our species has always expressed and received a sense of meaning. Ever since the birth of human consciousness on Earth, people have represented their intuitions of meaning through the medium of stories. In myths, epics, ballads, dramas, odysseys, histories, and other narrative forms humans have expressed their sense of how things hold together. Now, as it turns out, science itself is giving us a grand new story, the epic of evolution and the larger cosmic drama. A narrative, however, is something that begs to be read synthetically, not analytically. To read a story means to look for narrative coherence, not for mechanical or architectural elegance. So on the question of evolution, the primary point of interaction between theology and science is not the notion of design, which attracts the constricted scrutiny of both evolutionary naturalists and ID proponents. Rather, convergence looks for religious meaning primarily in the drama of nature. Focusing only on design—in the manner of ID and evolutionary naturalism—is a theological dead end.

Furthermore, convergence is not at all satisfied with contrast's casual conjecture that chance may not really exist or that it is a disguise for our human ignorance of some larger divine plan. In our opinion the accidents in evolution and natural history are quite real and dramatically necessary. An element of contingency, spontaneity, and unpredictability is an indispensable aspect of any real drama, including the drama of life. Chance is neither absurdity, as conflict supposes, nor illusion, as contrast believes. Rather, chance in evolution is essential for life's being the drama it is. Theologically the existence of chance is what we should expect if the story of life is to be consistent with our trust in a caring and promising God who keeps the future open. And if God is infinite love, as our traditions maintain, we should acknowledge that love does not coerce. Love allows the beloved to be and become itself. This means that God grants to creation, life, and human history room for spontaneity or indeterminacy and—in human persons—freedom to exist on their own and to be at least relatively self-determining.

God cares for the well-being of the world, but to convergence this well-being means having the time and space to become something *other* than God. The Abrahamic traditions all agree that what is created must be distinct from its creator. If creation were not distinct from God, it would be nothing more than an extension of God's own being. Hence it would not be a creation at all. There would be no room for the world to become something distinct from its creator. Becoming a world distinct from God requires, therefore, that the world possess an aspect of spontaneity that a perfectly designed product would lack.

So the randomness and openness in evolution are consistent with life's being a drama rather than a fixed set of designs. If God were a dictator or enforcer, we might expect the universe to be perfectly designed all at once in an initial moment of creative magic. And we might expect this perfectly designed world to remain essentially unchanged subsequently. If God were a supervising engineer in total control of things, as conflict demands, we would not expect the weird series of organisms that the drama of life puts on display as we move through geological and biological time scene by scene. We would not expect our idealized divine architect to manufacture the bizarre creatures of the Cambrian Explosion, the dinosaurs and reptiles, or the many other wild forms of life that seem so alien to our narrowly human sense of decent design. We would prefer that our divine magician construct the life-world once and for all according to our own blueprints of perfection.

Yet what a pallid world that would be compared to the one we have. Our human longing for an instantaneously finished world would suppress the drama, diversity, adventure, beauty—and, yes, tragedy—that evolution has wrought. Our perfectly designed cosmos would be more harmonious than the actual one, but it would have none of the dramatic grandeur that Darwin himself found so mysteriously compelling in his survey of life.

To convergence, the God of faith is not a magician but a creator,[8] and this creator is more interested in promoting freedom, adventure, and drama than freezing everything into undisturbed order from the start. Since God apparently loves stories, we are not at all surprised at evolution's strange and erratic pathways. The long drama of a universe that takes its time blossoming into life, intelligence, personality, moral aspiration, and religious longing is completely consonant with our faith's conviction that a truly providential love never forces but always takes the risk of allowing for spontaneity, surprise, freedom, and adventure.

In the century and a half since Darwin published the *Origin*, scientists have continued to find out things about the natural world that may not be consistent with innocent notions of divine design. The world of living things lacks the perfectly engineered mechanisms expected by ID proponents. Yet the relatively recent discovery of an unfinished cosmic story, including the drama of life's evolution, corresponds very well with the self-giving creative love and promises of the God of our faith traditions. God calls not only Abraham but also the whole universe into a new future. God's opening up of the future is the ultimate theological explanation of evolution. Moreover, God surprisingly and generously longs for all creatures, and not just humans, to share the work of creation. God gives to creatures a significant role, indeed a partnership in the ongoing drama of creation. God renounces any will to fashion creation all at once in the mode of perfect engineering and architecture. To do so would close the world off from having any real future. It would also preclude the emergence of human freedom.

From the perspective of convergence, let us add, the story of faith itself is part of the larger drama of life on Earth. Faith is an attempt by conscious personal beings to adapt to their ultimate environment, the infinite mystery of God. Because this infinite mystery forever evades complete comprehension, religious representations of God never quite "fit." So in our attempts to adapt more closely to our ultimate environment there will always be an ongoing restlessness, a persistent discontent with the religious and theological status quo — even, perhaps, a certain kind of "atheism." Religions too are subject to a kind of evolutionary selection and life cycle. The convergence approach proposes that our ultimate environment — what we refer to as "God" — continually sifts, sorts, and "judges" our religious symbols and myths, allowing us to let go of any religious projections that are not adaptive to an inexhaustible freedom, future, and love.

Serious atheism, as distinct from the shallow contemporary versions based on a self-contradictory scientism, is part of this adventure of letting go of maladaptive images of God. So we suggest that the often tumultuous drama of faith on Earth, along with all the wild wanderings of life at large, corresponds well with the Abrahamic understanding of an adventurous and loving God "who makes all things new."[9] We find it hard to reconcile our belief in a God of infinite love and promise with any other kind of universe than the one implied by Darwin's vision of life evolving.

CHAPTER 4

Do Miracles Really Happen?

CONFLICT

No, miracles don't happen. People who believe in God trick themselves into thinking they do. Jews, Christians, and Muslims believe God answers prayers and acts in the world. But where is the evidence? The word miracle means a violation of the laws that govern the physical world, but science has never observed any such exceptions. Albert Einstein, we noted earlier, correctly ruled out any plausible place for a personal God who answers prayers. To respond to prayers or perform miracles in the world, God would have to suspend the regulations that run the universe, but such exceptions would make a mockery of our belief in the absolute consistency of the laws of nature on which science is based.

The Christian Gospels tell you that Jesus walked on water, multiplied loaves and fishes, and rose from the dead. Yet anyone who knows how the natural world works cannot take any of this seriously. The gospel stories and other religious accounts of miracles are wishful thinking and nothing more. Scientific method alone can put you in touch with the real world, and the real world is lawful through and through. Nature is completely obedient to the changeless principles of chemistry and physics. These immutable routines can be clearly represented in mathematical terms, and the equations allow no swerving from predictability. No room exists for a divine miracle worker to interrupt or change the rules that govern the natural world.

Consequently, you need to face the fact that religious accounts of miracles are pure fiction. Even if you believe in them with all your heart, science allows no exceptions to the rigorous dictates of nature. If being scientific means denying miracles and God's existence, then so be it. For some people such a loss might bring sadness, but we take solace in knowing that we have faced reality without blinking. Falling back on belief in miracles seems cowardly by comparison. Our naturalist vision is inseparable from a sense of tragedy, we admit, but we would rather live without hope than wallow in illusions.

Our rejection of miracles is tied closely also to our denial that there can be divinely inspired scriptures. It is hard to understand how even educated people still believe that the Bible or the Qur'an could have been "inspired" by God. To scientifically informed people these allegedly sacred writings, though at times lyrical and aesthetically attractive, must seem mostly crude, ignorant, and self-contradictory. As Christopher Hitchens, the late journalist and atheist, points out, the Christian Gospels of Matthew and Luke can't even agree on the historical facts surrounding the birth of Jesus. "Either the gospels are in some sense literal truth," Hitchens observes, "or the whole thing is essentially a fraud and perhaps an immoral one at that."[1]

Richard Dawkins and his friend Daniel Dennett are justifiably dismayed that after Darwin many educated people take the idea of biblical inspiration seriously even though the Bible has nothing to say about evolution and other scientific discoveries. Similarly, the philosopher Sam Harris rightly laments the fact that believers pay any attention at all to their scriptures in the age of science. If the Bible is "written by God," Harris inquires, why is it not "the richest source of mathematical insight humanity has ever known"? If the Bible is inspired by God, why doesn't it give us reliable scientific information? Why do people still enshrine it as the source of significant revelation?[2]

Not all representatives of our conflict position, we must point out, follow the biblical literalism of Harris, Hitchens, and Dawkins. Nevertheless, we all agree that no evidence exists of a miracle-working supernatural reality breaking into the tightly woven fabric of nature. Moreover, we deny that divine inspiration has shaped the all-too-human ideas presented by allegedly sacred writings. Things that seem miraculous can now be fully explained by scientific laws, and "inspired" scriptures turn out to be no more than culturally narrow imaginings motivated by wishful thinking. Close scientific analysis shows that nature is governed totally by impersonal physical laws. And careful historical study demonstrates that the sacred scriptures of Jews, Christians, and Muslims are so full of factual inaccuracies and groundless conjecture that no self-respecting scientifically educated person can take them seriously.

CONTRAST

The simplistic critique just presented by the contemporary partisans of conflict (including the New Atheists) misunderstands what a mature faith or a reasonable theology means by "miracles." Likewise it completely misses the meaning of scriptural revelation and divine inspiration. Miracles are not violations of nature at all, nor is belief in biblical inspiration by God a contradiction of the fact that scriptures are also human compositions. Let us look first at miracles and then take up the question of scriptural inspiration.

We accept the fact that nature's laws are predictable and unbending. So we are willing to embrace the modern scientific understanding of the physical universe as a closed continuum of cause-and-effect relationships.[3] We accept the notion that the natural world operates according to inviolable natural laws. However, for us a miracle is not an event that suspends, bends, or breaks the laws of nature in the slightest way. *Miracle* means "something to wonder about," and faith in the miraculous does not contradict the scientific search for regularity and lawfulness in the natural world. By a "miracle" we mean something much more dramatic—and much more interesting—than a suspension of the laws of physics, chemistry, and biology. The real miracles, indeed the only ones worth talking about at all, are the improbable transformations that occasionally lead a person from a life of mediocrity to one of authenticity and goodness. This is the only kind of miracle we are concerned with, so conflict only trivializes miracles by defining them as violations of the predictable routines of nature.

Something dramatically miraculous, and unpredictable, occurs when a person, against all expectations, undergoes a conversion from a life of despair to a life of hope and trust. Something truly "to be wondered at" happens when an irresponsible and selfish individual turns around and takes up a life of gratitude and self-giving. Such significant events of grace are not interruptions of nature. Rather, they are interruptions of banality and mediocrity. As far as contrast is concerned, this remarkable kind of transformation is the true theological meaning of miracles.

There is no way to measure or mathematically quantify such momentous events. They remain completely beyond the scrutiny of science. The way in which God works in the created world is not by breaking laws of nature but by quietly attracting human *subjects* to trust in the infinite meaning, truth, goodness, and beauty that have always embraced the universe but that remain completely beyond the horizon of scientism. God is the encompassing reality in whom "we live and move and have our being" (Acts 17:28). That which is deepest and most real—God, in other words—eludes comprehension by the finite human mind, and especially by the scientific mind.

The kind of awareness that contrast refers to as "faith" is nothing like the objectifying control sought by scientific experimentation. God can never be an object but is always a subject. So nothing less than an interpersonal kind of experience is essential to understanding miracles. The experience of faith is that of allowing oneself to be changed radically by a love that is infinitely larger than we are. We look for evidence of divine influence and presence not in the mundane data of scientific inquiry, but in the shining forth of joy and goodness that a transformed personal life can radiate. The kind of evidence that scientism holds up as the standard of truth is cheap by comparison. We are not disparaging scientific inquiry in any way, and we fully accept well-established scientific ideas. However, we notice a sharp difference or *contrast* between the "transformative" evidence on which faith in the miraculous is grounded and the publicly accessible "spectator" evidence on which science is based.

Countless people have testified to the wondrous renewal of their own lives that accompanies the call to faith. They have found that faith launches them onto a journey of discovery that makes the adventure of scientific inquiry pale in comparison. Many great scientists have themselves undertaken the journey of faith as well as that of science. They have never for a moment thought of their faith as contradictory to their science, nor have they thought of science as an impediment to religious transformation. The goal of each respective journey is distinct but compatible with the other. Moreover, the transition from an irresponsible life to one of selflessness requires not the slightest violation of the laws of nature. Indeed, the predictable and invariant operations of chemical, biological, and neurological processes are necessary conditions for the kind of personal transformation we are talking about. When a person of faith confesses, "I once was blind but now I see," there is no violation of nature's laws.

A good example of what we mean by a miraculous transformation is the journey from a state of mind shaped by scriptural literalism to a more serious way of reading sacred texts. We emphasize this point because conflict's rejection of scriptural "inspiration," our second topic, generally stems from the same mentality that wants miracles to fall within the field of spectator evidence. "Literalism" remains the characteristic mind-set not only of religious fundamentalists but also of many (though not all) devotees of scientism. Literalism is the result of a refusal to undergo the radical personal transformation required to "see" the deeper levels of meaning beneath the plain sense of our scriptures.

Literalism has been around ever since great literature first appeared. It occurs especially when readers stubbornly refuse to face the truly challenging meanings that inspired authors' attempt to communicate through mythic, symbolic, metaphorical, ironic, and paradoxical modes of expression. Today literalism often takes the form of treating ancient texts that could not possibly have had any scientific intentions, as though they should be sources of modern scientific information. This literalist expectation, we repeat, is characteristic not only of religious fundamentalists but also of many devotees of scientism who espouse the conflict position.

The New Atheists are the best example we can find of literalism's invasion of intellectual culture today. Dennett, Dawkins, Hitchens, and Harris, along with many other educated people, devoutly believe that scientific method is the only reliable road to truth. For them scientism is the height of intellectual sophistication. To contrast, however, it is intellectually shocking that each of the New Atheists reads the Bible as though it should respond to scientific curiosity and be judged by scientific standards. Along with their creationist adversaries, the New Literalists completely miss the transformative meaning, for example, in the accounts of origins in the biblical Book of Genesis. They lampoon biblical creation stories for failing to give us the kind of cosmological and biological information that can compete with modern science. In doing so, they completely avoid the challenge to new life that lies beneath the literal sense of the scriptural narratives of origins.

Contrast, on the other hand, reads the biblical creation stories as attempts by our religious ancestors to arouse in readers a sense of gratitude, humility, and hope. The last thing we expect from the scriptures is a picture of nature that either confirms or competes with modern scientific understanding. Biblical accounts of origins contain a highly nuanced set of religious meanings that have nourished people of faith for centuries. Literalism, however, dodges these meanings altogether. It fails to see, for example, that Genesis is responding not to scientific questions but to the deeper human concern, for example, about why there is anything at all, or whether there is an ultimate reason for trust and hope (see chapter 5).

No doubt the transition from literalism to mature faith is difficult, but sometimes this miracle occurs, and we hope it will happen to you if it hasn't happened already. Literalism, along with a shallow sense of scriptural inspiration, is a way of taking flight from the real significance of biblical texts. If you are obsessed, for example, with the question of whether the miracle stories in the scriptures are scientifically verifiable, you too have missed their point. Maybe you have been tempted at times by the cheap allure of contemporary religious or scientific literalism. Perhaps you are impressed by the letter-for-letter approach of Sam Harris, who is incredulous that the ancient holy books tell us nothing about things like evolutionary biology or Big Bang cosmology. Or maybe you have nodded your assent when

Christopher Hitchens condemns the evangelists Matthew and Luke for failing to agree on the historical details surrounding the birth of Jesus. We hope you will come to see that theologically transformed sensibilities ignore such surface disagreements and attend instead to the call to faith and hope that these artfully composed chapters of scripture bring to expression.

To sum up, then, contrast never looks to sacred scriptures for scientific information. In the words often attributed to theologian Reinhold Niebuhr, we take our sacred writings seriously, not literally. Did the Red Sea literally form walls of water to let the Israelites pass through? Did manna literally fall from heaven or water actually spring from rocks in the desert wanderings of Israel? Did Jesus literally walk on water and rise from the dead? Without faith, even if such wonders physically interrupted the normal course of nature, they would do very little to transform your life. Maybe this is why the Gospels tell us that Jesus was unable to work miracles among those who refused to open themselves to his message of radical hope, love of neighbor, and trust in God. His speaking so often in parables instead of plain speech indicates his own longing to overcome the paralysis of literalism.

What our scriptures are mostly about is transformation, not information. Genuine faith is not a state of believing in divine interruptions of nature, as though the influence of God could ever be the object of scientific comprehension. This is a childish way of thinking about faith. Instead, faith is a matter of undergoing a profound change of one's whole life in the presence of an infinite love and freedom that radically transcends nature. Scriptural accounts of the miraculous are not about events that interrupt the laws of nature but about a divine calling that interrupts the profanity of our lives.

CONVERGENCE

We agree with contrast that both religious and New Atheist literalism completely misunderstand what miracle stories are about. Nevertheless, in our opinion the contrast approach does not address all the relevant issues in the conversation about miracles. The perceptive reader will have noticed that contrast still shares with scientific materialism an obsolete understanding of nature and nature's laws. Contrast concedes too much to the mechanistic and deterministic understanding of the physical universe that thrived during the early modern period and that still underlies much contemporary naturalism. Both conflict and contrast naïvely assume that nature is a dictatorship run by inviolable laws and that nature's laws are comparable to a system of legal enforcement.

The convergence approach, however, interprets the laws of nature as enabling conditions rather than crippling constraints. The rigid understanding of physical laws presupposed by conflict implies that all events in the natural world conform to ironclad regulations inscribed indelibly in physical processes from of old. This deterministic picture of the world is one in which human freedom finds no home and into which divine influence cannot enter. By taking the classical principles of inertia and momentum too literally, mechanism/determinism offers a picture of nature in which nothing truly new can ever happen. To most adherents of scientism, the prison of nature is forever hemmed in by fateful necessity. Everything that will ever happen in the physical universe is already embedded in the physics of the early universe and simply needs time to unfold. Nature, as Peter Atkins, a champion of scientism and materialism, puts it, is "simplicity masquerading as complexity."[4]

Contrast unfortunately follows conflict too closely in assuming that nature is a closed network of lawful occurrences. It differs from conflict by making a separate space for human freedom and divine action in a mysterious sphere of reality that somehow exists apart from nature. Contrast rightly acknowledges that what is most real lies beyond the grasp of the human mind, but in doing so it holds fast to the antiquated view that the physical universe itself is completely subject to deterministic laws. For contrast there is no room for freedom in nature itself, only in a world of personal "subjectivity" that transcends nature.

Our convergence approach, though, takes advantage of recent developments in science to portray nature as an ongoing story in which surprising new occurrences, such as the emergence of life, mind, and freedom, can occur as part of a still unfolding universe. Contrast, as you will see throughout this book, is content to take the view that we humans are not really a part of the natural world. Contrast allows that our bodily existence is continuous with nature, but it makes a separate place outside of nature for human subjectivity and freedom, the very core of personal existence. As you saw in the preceding section of this chapter, contrast allows that miracles can occur in the hidden realm of human freedom and subjectivity. In that arena, inaccessible to the objectifying gaze of science, a deeply personal encounter with God can take place and a miracle of personal transformation may then occur. However, the price contrast pays for this isolation of personal subjects from nature is that it sets the non-human physical world adrift in a sea of pointlessness.

Convergence, however, assumes that the human mind and human freedom are just as much a part of the natural world as rocks and rivers. For reasons that we can lay out only gradually throughout this book, convergence rejects the assumption that the laws of nature are all determining and that they are contrary to the existence of real freedom and personality. At the same time, our understanding of nature allows that God can act powerfully in the universe without violating any laws of nature. We don't pretend, though, to understand all that is meant by the term *miracle*. Our claim is simply that biblical accounts of divine activity and the resurrection of Jesus are ways by which faith affirms that something of transformative significance is going on in the whole *universe*, and not just in our private personal existence.

To allow for this more cosmic view of the miraculous we assume that the laws of nature are enabling conditions rather than iron-rail imprisonment. And where contrast speaks of miracles as hidden personal transformation, convergence highlights the greater miracle of cosmic transformation that science itself has enabled us to wonder about. Once we realize that the cosmos is a still unfolding drama rather than just an interesting collection of things in space, it becomes possible to speak of a momentous transformation going on in the entirety of God's creation and not just in the hidden arena of personal existence.

From the perspective of Abrahamic faith, miracles are inseparable from the more basic themes of promise and hope. The purpose of miracle stories is to awaken in us a sense of trust that God is doing something new (Isa 43:19 and Rev 21:5), not just in ourselves but also in the whole of creation. If we understand a miracle only as a local display of magic, we have lost touch with its cosmic significance.

How, though, can we reconcile faith's trust that the world is always open to unpredictable, even miraculous, transformation with science's sense that everything also obeys the inviolable laws of nature? Sometimes, to get across a new point of view we have to start with a change of metaphors. We can make both intellectual and theological room for miracles of transformation if we revise the terminology scientists have been using to describe nature. Specifically, let us think of nature's predictable and habitual routines not in terms of the ideas of law enforcement and imprisonment but as analogous to grammatical rules. In view of the fact that science has now shown nature to be a still unfinished narrative, let us exchange the juridical metaphor of nature's *laws* for that of nature's *grammar*. Likewise let us drop the outdated metaphor of nature as a set of mechanisms and adopt the richer metaphor of nature as a *drama*. Once we make these metaphorical adjustments, all the questions pertaining to science and faith, including those about miracles, take on a new look.

Ever since the late eighteenth century, discoveries in the fields of geology, evolutionary biology, and cosmology have increasingly forced scientists to understand nature as a still unfinished story or drama. And just as a Shakespearian drama may unfold in surprising ways without being unfaithful to syntax and grammatical rules, so also the universe unfolds in novel and unpredictable ways at the level of dramatic meaning while remaining completely predictable at the level of its grammatical constraints—or what conflict and contrast refer to as "nature's laws." A piece of literature can express a completely new and unpredictable meaning not by violating grammatical rules but by sticking to them. So can the cosmos.

In literature the writing of a drama or novel, regardless of the direction in which its meaning or set of meanings unfolds, always employs and obeys the same set of grammatical rules. Notice, however, that the rules of grammar are not prison walls but instead enabling conditions that allow for the expression of an indeterminate range of meanings. Whether one is writing fiction or nonfiction, the same set of syntactical regulations apply. Yet each piece of writing can be totally new and unprecedented. Grammar, rigid though it is, does not prevent surprising new meanings from appearing in speech and writing.

It is in the context of a still unfinished cosmic *story* of transformation that theology may speak of miracles without in any way contradicting science. We don't maintain that this is the only appropriate way to think of miracles theologically. Rather, our convergence approach simply acknowledges that the meaning of miracle stories in our holy books is to awaken us to the prospect that something new is breaking into the world as a whole and not just into our private subjectivity.

Conflict, dominated by the myth of scientism, understands nature as a collection of objects blindly bumping against or attracting one another physically in space and time. Following the dictates of scientific materialism, conflict interprets nature as driven by nothing more at bottom than unchanging and imprisoning physical laws. Such an outlook, however, is comparable to saying that a Shakespearean drama is nothing more than the expression of the invariant grammatical rules that underlie it.

To be sure, inflexible grammatical rules do "generate" every sentence and scene in a Shakespearean drama. But obviously there is much more going on in the drama than expertise in the rules of grammar can ever discover. Otherwise you would only have to go to a grammarian rather than a literary critic to understand a great piece of literature. Doing so, of course, would be silly. Likewise, consulting the expert in physics to find out whether the universe has a meaning or meanings is equally silly. There is much more going on in the cosmic story than chemistry and physics alone can illuminate. For example, there is the wondrous cosmic awakening to consciousness now taking place in our universe after nearly 14 billion years of dormancy. But scientific understanding of the mindless "laws" of physics and chemistry can tell you very little about any possible new meaning in this most dramatic epoch of cosmic transformation.[5]

Look at it this way. Each of us has to adhere scrupulously to the same set of grammatical rules if we expect our oral and written expressions to be intelligible to others. And yet we don't feel inhibited by these grammatical constraints. On the contrary, rigorous and unchanging grammatical rules expand, rather than reduce, the manifold ways in which our sentences can signify. Accordingly, you can safely predict that every intelligible essay you write in the future will adhere to the same inviolable set of grammatical regulations that you are using right now. Grammatical rules prescribe that the verb of every sentence must agree with its subject, that double negatives and sentence fragments should be avoided, and so on, but these rules don't inhibit your creativity. Just the opposite. Likewise, the regularity of the laws of nature is completely consistent with new and unexpected turns in the ongoing narrative transformation of what we call creation. If some of these events seem miraculous, it is not because they are violating the laws of nature, but because they are bringing something truly new into the sphere of being.

We now realize, in any case, that scientific laws are so abstract that they tell us very little about the concrete uniqueness or novelty of things that happen in the natural world or about any possible meaning in nature as such. In addition to the mathematical coherence that science seeks in its understanding of the laws of physics or chemistry, there is also a *narrative coherence* that faith and theology are seeking as they read the universe story. So there is no real conflict between faith and science. Understanding nature's laws as enabling conditions rather than fateful necessity allows us to interpret the mighty acts of God narrated by the Abrahamic traditions in a way that is completely consistent with scientific understanding on the one hand and the requirements of faith on the other.

Miracle stories and accounts of divine action are ways of expressing faith's conviction that something of special importance is going on in creation. But this dimension of importance cannot be grasped by science any more than studying grammar can comprehend Shakespeare's meaning. And just as Shakespeare's creative inventiveness does not disturb the predictable functioning of grammar, so also even the most dramatic developments in the story of cosmic transformation—especially the emergence of life, mind, freedom, and the miracle of love—do not interrupt the physical rules regulating atomic and molecular motion.

Unfortunately, the modern idea of scientific laws has made nature seem more like a lockup than liberation. The outdated legalistic metaphor still undergirds conflict's debunking of faith's expectation that surprising and unpredictable events can occur as the universe story continues into the future. To the mechanist the emergence of life and mind, for example, is nothing to wonder about since it is all just the playing out of physical necessity. Unfortunately, contrast also concedes too much to this shallow picture of what's going on in the universe. To convergence, however, once we realize that nature is a still unfolding story, the predictable "laws" of nature are no longer an oppressive set of restrictions. Instead they are grammatical conditions for the arrival of surprising new events and new meanings in the cosmic story. Viewing nature's routines as grammatical rules rather than draconian dictates allows for an endless reservoir of yet untapped meanings to be actualized as the cosmic story continues to unfurl.

The dramatic character of nature, therefore, now allows us to consolidate the theme of miracle with that of scriptural inspiration. Both "miracle" and "inspiration" are expressions of faith's sense that something radically new is breaking into the world. Convergence, therefore, views nature and scripture as two strands of a single inspired narrative. Before science discovered the cosmic story, people of faith thought we could learn about God by reading two separate books, the book of scripture and the book of nature. Theologians hoped the two books would not contradict each other, but reconciling them was often difficult.

Theologians and scientists both thought that perhaps they could find in nature's "design" a bridge between the two books. As we saw in the previous chapter, however, after Darwin nature does not seem to have been designed very carefully. Cells and organisms have been cobbled together haphazardly over an enormous amount of time, and most experiments have not worked. Only a few living beings have been adaptive enough to survive and reproduce. There have been tragedy and loss along with creativity. Evolution has at last given rise to consciousness, freedom, and the capacity for love, but it has also let into the universe an unprecedented capacity for suffering and evil.

Nevertheless, because the story of life and the universe is a work in progress, we may keep looking for a future coherence on the horizon up ahead. If the universe is a story, faith looks for its meaning not by fixing its attention on transitional instances of "engineering" or biological design, but by *waiting* for a narrative coherence that at present remains out of sight. The universe remains unfinished, so hope is still possible. It is their shared openness to the future that allows us now to merge our two books into one. The inspired books of our faith traditions, diverse though they may be, witness to a God who opens up not just our hearts but the whole universe to the creation of new meaning up ahead.

For centuries people everywhere have told stories and derived meaning from them without understanding formally the grammatical rules that make storytelling possible. The discovery and articulation of grammatical rules or "generative grammar" by modern linguistics is illuminating and interesting too. But even a sophisticated contemporary understanding of linguistics cannot tell you the meaning of a play or story. Comparably, nature has always been an unfolding story, but the recent scientific formulation of the laws of chemistry, physics, and biology will tell you nothing about any transformative meaning that may be coming to expression in this greatest of all epics. The quest for cosmic meaning leaves plenty of room for faith and theology in the age of science. And our sense of hope and expectation no more conflicts with science than the meaning of a story conflicts with the grammatical rules that allow it to be told.

CHAPTER 5

Was the Universe Created?

CONFLICT

No. The universe was not created. There is no evidence that any deity brought it into existence. We have no reason for believing that it has its origin in anything beyond itself. Since nature is all there is, there can be no creator, no divine providence, no cosmic purpose. As you will read from our adversaries following, people of faith believe that the universe had a beginning in time and that a beneficent creator brought it into existence. Scientific understanding of the universe, however, provides no reason for believing in God or creation.

Scientists have now gathered evidence that our universe originated around 13.7 billion years ago, and the idea that the universe had a beginning might seem at first to support the biblical accounts of creation. The Book of Genesis starts out, after all, with the words: "In the beginning when God created the heavens and the earth...." Admittedly creation by God was a radically new idea in the world of ancient thought. For centuries, thinkers outside of the Abrahamic traditions had assumed that matter is eternal, but they were probably wrong about this. Big Bang cosmology seems to support the claim that our universe is temporally finite. The natural world, as we realize today, has been around for a long time, but not forever. So you might be tempted to ask how the universe suddenly popped into existence abruptly out of apparent nothingness nearly 14 billion years ago. Isn't the idea of an omnipotent creator a reasonable explanation after all?

Conflict sees no need to jump to such a conclusion. Even if the Big Bang universe did have a definite beginning in time, it may be only one of many universes spawned by an eternal "mother universe." Maybe our Big Bang universe is only one of an innumerable throng of universes that pass in and out of existence. Or perhaps our own universe is part of a bouncing series of cosmic expansions and contractions, the record of which is wiped out prior to each new beginning. Or it may be that our universe simply came into existence without any cause beyond itself. Nothing in science has yet ruled out these possibilities, so we have no need for the conjectures of theology.

The idea that our own universe had a beginning is supported partly by the fact that it is still expanding. If we imaginatively travel back in time, reversing the lines of cosmic expansion, we eventually arrive at a point long ago when the whole universe was a tiny, dense, and extremely hot speck no larger than an atom's nucleus.[1] Nearly 14 billion years ago this infinitesimal entity abruptly burst forth in what scientists now call the "Big Bang." By going back in time, therefore, science brings us close to the originating edge of the cosmos. And what does science find lurking on the other side of this boundary? What was there "before" the Big Bang? Nothing whatsoever, at least as far as science can tell.

Not only the evidence of cosmic expansion, but also Einstein's general theory of relativity (1917), lends credibility to the idea of a Big Bang universe. Yet even Einstein at first could not believe the universe was changing dramatically over time. He had clung to the ancient belief that the material universe had existed pretty much in the same state forever. The idea that the universe had a beginning in time seemed to violate his firm conviction that the laws of nature are eternal and inviolable. A true beginning would imply that the laws of nature had not existed forever, and Einstein could not accept such an idea because it would place science on too shaky a foundation. Science, he thought, has to assume that nature's fundamental laws have existed eternally.

However, the Russian mathematician Alexander Friedmann and the physicist Georges Lemaître, a Belgian Catholic priest, informed Einstein that his newly formulated theory of general relativity implied a dynamic rather than an eternally unchanging cosmos. But Einstein, the most famous scientist of the twentieth century, was not ready to accept a universe that had a beginning. He preferred instead a cosmos that extended back endlessly into the past and whose laws had no temporal beginning. Yet if the universe has existed forever, by now the coupling force of gravity would have brought all cosmic matter together into one big lump. Obviously this hasn't occurred, because matter remains distributed far and wide in the universe. So if the universe has existed forever, Einstein thought, there must be a hidden force—a cosmological constant—that holds back the pull of gravity. He artificially adjusted his theory to make a place for this supposed counterforce. There must be, he surmised, an undetected power of repulsion that keeps cosmic bodies apart during all eternity, preventing the universe from collapsing onto itself.

However, after conferring with Lemaître and the American astronomer Edwin Hubble, among others, Einstein was forced to change his mind and abandon the idea of a changeless universe. Hubble and his assistants had observed that the light radiating from a number of galaxies was measurably shifted toward the red end of the light spectrum. This "red shift" could only mean that the light waves emanating from the fleeing galaxies are longer than others and that the objects emitting them must be moving rapidly away from the observer and from one another. Evidently, then, the universe is expanding at an enormous rate of speed. Einstein, in a touching expression of scientific humility, admitted that he had been wrong. He finally accepted the evidence that our universe is still dynamically changing and hence cannot be eternal.

Misgivings about the Big Bang still lingered on for a time even after Hubble's discoveries. The Big Bang theory was given a considerable boost, however, when in 1965 scientists Robert Wilson and Arno Penzias discovered a low-temperature cosmic background microwave radiation that could only be interpreted as the afterglow of the Big Bang. This radiation was the clearest signal to date that a singular originating cosmic event had occurred billions of years earlier. It was now getting harder than ever to doubt that the universe had a beginning.

And yet, even after the background radiation was identified there remained a murmur of dissatisfaction. If the universe started off with a

Big Bang, why didn't it expand smoothly and uniformly in all directions? Observations show that in the wide universe, matter clusters more densely in some regions and more sparsely in others. Galaxies, stars, planets, gases, and other kinds of matter are distributed unevenly. To produce such a rough distribution of matter there must have been seeds of present cosmic irregularity even during the very earliest stages of its expansion. But where is the evidence that this unevenness existed in the early universe?

In the spring of 1992 measurements collected by a satellite called COBE, the Cosmic Background Explorer, signified that when the universe was still in its infancy there were already temperature differentiations in the primordial microwave radiation. Soon after it began, the cosmos had already exhibited a distinctively uneven or rippled character. Early pockets of temperature differentiation were the germs of the uneven universe we have today. So now, in the early twenty-first century, the Big Bang theory seems safe. Science, of course, is still far from understanding the universe completely. We still don't fully understand black holes, dark matter, and dark energy. And string theory suggests that the cosmos has many more dimensions than we had expected. In any case, it is still a safe scientific bet that the universe we live in had a beginning.

Nevertheless, the thought that our universe had a beginning does not demonstrate the existence of a creator. You may object. You may assume that if our universe had a beginning there is need for a creator who caused it to exist. Doesn't everything that comes into existence have to have a cause? Not necessarily. Simply acknowledging that the universe had a beginning is not the same as proving the existence of a first cause. Today quantum cosmology allows that the universe came into being out of *nothing*, without being caused or created. The cosmos may have had a beginning, but this does not mean it had a cause. New developments in physics allow us to think of the universe as coming into existence spontaneously, without any external influence whatsoever.[2]

How so? According to Big Bang theory and quantum physics, the universe at one time was about the size of a subatomic particle, and so we can assume that it behaved the way such particles do. The "virtual" particles of microphysics pass in and out of existence spontaneously. They are not "caused." Since the primitive universe was at one time subatomic in nature and size, it too could have come into existence without any determining cause. In the subatomic domain, virtual particles literally pop into existence from a vacuum. So it is conceivable that the primordial universe arose from *nothing*. The Big Bang itself was a spontaneous, uncaused vacuum fluctuation.[3] And so, if the universe had no external cause, why should we think it was created?

Proposing that the Big Bang universe never had a crisply defined temporal beginning, the renowned astrophysicist Stephen Hawking recently gave our conflict position a significant boost. Hawking submits that linear, irreversible time emerged only gradually out of a space-time matrix, so there may well have been no clearly defined first moment after all, and therefore no first cause either. And if the cosmos had no true beginning, what need is there for a creator?[4] The universe just happened.

CONTRAST

To people of faith the Genesis account of creation is much more than a story intended to satisfy cosmological curiosity about how the universe began. The Bible's meaning goes much deeper than science can discover, for it speaks directly to a common human concern about whether there are any realistic grounds for hope that our lives have a meaning. At stake in any discussion of the theology of creation is whether there is an ultimate reason for our trusting in reality and the significance of our own existence. The scientific naturalists of whom you have just been reading miss the point of faith's doctrine of creation altogether: they mistake a theological belief for a scientific theory. It is typical of conflict, as we have already noted, to confuse the task of theology and the meaning of scripture with the business of scientific inquiry.

Nevertheless, contrast agrees with conflict that Big Bang physics provides no new support for faith and theology. Many believers in

God wrongly look for theological implications in scientific discoveries, but this only leads to confusion followed by conflict. Contrast's strategy is to differentiate theology so sharply from science that no opportunity for the two to clash will ever arise. Contrast has great respect for both science and theology, and so it refuses to compromise the integrity of either by forging superficial alliances.

No matter how many new insights scientific inquiry will harvest in the future, there are certain questions it can never deal with. Among these are, Why does anything exist at all? Why is the universe intelligible? Why should I seek truth? What is the meaning of my life? Is there a point to the universe? Why act responsibly? Science by definition must not even attempt to answer such questions or else it will fade into a kind of pseudo-theology. Since scientists are human persons like the rest of us, they may personally ask such big questions, but the questions do not permit scientific answers. There can be no spectator evidence or quantitatively precise answers to allay our religious preoccupations.

So even if Big Bang cosmology has won the day in science, this fact provides no new comfort to those of us who already believe in the creativity and renewing power of God. We shall never tie the plausibility of our theology of creation to anything as unsteady as the shifting sands of natural science. We are impressed scientifically but not theologically with Big Bang cosmology, even if the latter seems at first to support biblical accounts of the world's beginnings. If we read in tomorrow's newspaper that Big Bang theory is scientifically mistaken, it will not disturb our faith and theology at all. Theologically speaking, therefore, we are no more enthusiastic about Big Bang cosmology than about the Steady State cosmology of Fred Hoyle, for example, or any other cosmological theories that will arise in the future. No cosmology, new or old, has any business answering religious questions, just as theology has no business providing scientific information.

What then is the theology of divine creation all about? It has multiple meanings, but we need only concentrate here on the fact that it responds to the question of why anything exists at all. This is not a scientific question, and science has no answer for it, as even most scientific skeptics agree.[5] The theological notion of creation is not about physical and chronological beginnings but about the wondrous fact that anything exists at all. All perishable beings, including us humans, depend for their existence on something beyond themselves. So why not the universe too? The doctrine of divine creation is a response to the question whether the universe can be its own explanation. Unlike science, however, theology does not look for a first physical cause of the universe because such a cause would be part of a causal series that is itself finite. Instead theology looks for a "sufficient reason" why any finite beings exist at all, including the immense, but still finite, body of things we call the universe. It looks for what theologian Paul Tillich calls the "Ground of Being."[6] We call this Ground of Being by the name "God." And we are confident that science has found nothing to make this idea untenable. Nor will it ever do so in the future.

Big Bang theory, we have no doubt, is a scientifically fruitful way of understanding the physical universe, but it should not be confused with the doctrine of creation. For instead of giving us any useful scientific information, the doctrine of creation is concerned to make us aware that the universe is a free gift of divine love, regardless of how it began or even whether it had a beginning in time. Creation theology seeks to arouse in us a disposition of gratitude for the marvel that the universe exists at all. Nothing that Big Bang cosmology or any other cosmological speculation tells us about the universe can make its existence, or our own, any more wondrous than it already is.

Creation theology also implies that a God who can bring the universe into existence out of nothing can surely also raise the dead and provide a permanent meaning to our lives. So it is irrelevant to genuine faith whether the universe began in time or not. Any kind of universe would still require an eternal, transcendent Ground and source of its continuing existence. Even if the universe *began* to exist in time, its existence here and now still depends on God's sustaining it continually. Our creation theology's focus is on the world's sheer *existence*, not its chronological origins. Even though Stephen Hawking deserves our scientific respect, he is no theologian. He completely misses the mark when he claims that if the universe had no clear beginning it had no need for a creator. The theology of creation, as the great thirteenth-century philosopher Thomas Aquinas taught us, is not dependent on the supposition that the universe had a temporal beginning at all, even though Aquinas thought that it did. For even an eternal universe would still depend for its existence on the infinitely resourceful self-giving love that people of faith call God.

Finally, quantum cosmological speculation about the spontaneous origins of the universe does nothing to overturn belief in the world's creation by God. For even if the infinitesimal early universe erupted spontaneously out of a quantum vacuum, the truly important question remains: Why are there beings at all, including quantum vacuums and virtual particles? To call a vacuum by the name "nothing" is one of the word tricks that scientific skeptics at times resort to in their futile attempts to discredit theistic faith.[7] To identify a quantum vacuum or the original cosmological symmetry of mathematical "zero" with "nothingness" goes beyond silliness. No matter how mathematically or physically subtle the initial cosmic conditions may have been, they still enjoyed some mode of *being*. Otherwise physicists couldn't refer to them at all or write elaborate mathematical equations about them. Theologically speaking, it is the sheer existence of things that evokes our sense of religious wonder.

CONVERGENCE

Once again the contrast approach provides a clear alternative to conflict's narrow scientism. It rightly resists the strong temptation to identify the Big Bang with divine creation. Unfortunately, its severe separation of science from theology is on display here once again, cutting off the prospect of fruitful dialogue. Our convergence position, as usual, claims that the large body of modern and recent scientific discoveries always has theological implications. Science, we agree, is forever changing, but some scientific ideas are likely to stand the test of time indefinitely. It is not likely, for example, that the Copernican theory of the heavens will ever be overturned or that the hypothesis of a flat Earth will ever regain scientific currency. It is almost as unlikely that Big Bang cosmology will be overturned, even though scientists will continually refine and improve it in the future.

So we look for points of convergence and interaction between lasting scientific ideas such as Big Bang cosmology on the one hand and creation theology on the other. Convergence does not base theology directly on contemporary cosmology, but it wagers that current scientific understanding of the universe can help enliven theology in important new ways. Consequently, convergence takes advantage of Big Bang cosmology in its reflections on the biblical accounts of creation.[8]

We believe Big Bang cosmology is significant theologically for at least four reasons. First and foremost, it has been Big Bang science above all that allows us to think of the universe as a *story*. During much of the modern age we were unaware of the dramatic character of nature. Partly due to the ideas of the philosopher Immanuel Kant, the universe seemed to be merely a background for human existence and action. It was primarily a staging area for the human drama, not a sweeping set of events that the human mind could focus on directly by way of scientific method.[9]

Prior to Einstein and Big Bang cosmology, the universe had become virtually lost to modern theology. Humans did not realize how closely each of us is linked to the story of the universe. Contrast tries to convince you that even now you don't really belong to the universe. Contrast is interested in the drama of personal transformation but not in the drama of cosmic transformation. To convergence, however, a major implication of Big Bang cosmology is that it invites us to understand ourselves as part of the larger cosmic story. The close narrative linkage of ourselves to nature has implications for how we may now think about God, human destiny, and the whole of creation. Throughout the rest of this book we spell out some of these implications.

Second, and closely related to our first point, Big Bang cosmology is theologically important for the simple reason that it presents us with a universe that is *still in the making*. Put theologically, the creation of the cosmos is far from finished. Especially as a result of its encounter with geology, evolutionary biology, and now cosmology, convergence takes seriously the fact that creation is still going on.

Why does this matter? It matters because all the big questions we humans have ever asked look different now that we realize we live in an unfinished universe. This applies especially to the perennial question of suffering and evil. For if the universe is still coming into being, we cannot expect it to be finished or perfectly designed at present. We cannot be totally surprised that it has a dark or tragic side. At the same time, however, an unfinished universe is open to having a continually new future. There is room for hope. Even though an unfinished universe is an imperfect universe, it may still be pregnant with surprising outcomes up ahead.

When combined with the idea of biological evolution, Big Bang cosmology implies that the world is new every day and that it still remains open to a creative future. As Teilhard de Chardin puts it, "Creation has never stopped. The creative act is one huge continual gesture, drawn out over the totality of time. It is still going on; and incessantly even if imperceptibly, the world is constantly emerging a little farther above nothingness."[10] The universe, in other words, may still become *more*. The universe is a place of hope and promise and thus a suitable habitat for Abrahamic faith. If you are asking why a creator would make an unfinished universe in the first place, think carefully about the alternative: An initially perfect creation would leave no room for a future. Everything would be fixed and finalized. There would be no opportunity for new things to happen. An initially perfect universe would leave no room for freedom either, because everything would be frozen in place forever. Nor would life even be possible, because life is a kind of striving that feeds off of the open future. To put it bluntly, there really is no theologically intelligible alternative to an initially unfinished universe.[11]

In our theological reflection on the openness of the future to new creation, we must also point out here that Big Bang cosmology decisively rules out any "eternal return of the same." This is the depressing notion (articulated especially by the nineteenth-century philosopher Friedrich Nietzsche) that if matter is eternal and the universe exists forever then every event must periodically repeat itself. And if every event repeats itself again and again, no matter how lengthy the interval between repetitions, there could be no completely open or indeterminate future. Sameness would be the final word. However, science has shown that the Big Bang universe is temporally irreversible, leaving the future open. In the large picture of things there is no going back, so the future will always be new. Today it seems clear to us that science is incompatible with the fatalism of ancient tragedy and modern materialism. The Big Bang universe is completely open to being understood in terms of the biblical theme of promise.

Third, Big Bang cosmology opens up *a place for human creativity* more explicitly than traditional theology was ever able to do. Science has now shown that the universe did not come into existence fully formed, so there is still work to be done. It is of utmost importance to convergence's understanding of human spirituality that human beings can contribute at least modestly to the ongoing creation of the cosmos. We are not passive puppets of fate. We have a chance to cooperate in making the world new, at least here on Earth. If the universe is still coming into being, this means that we can participate in the creative process and understand our human vocation in a way that prescientific theologies could never have enjoyed. The new sense of an unfinished universe opens up the future for human effort and achievement in a remarkably refreshing way. Science does make a difference to faith and theology!

Cosmologists of course speculate that eventually the Big Bang universe will end in a deep freeze and will no longer be able to sustain life as we know it. We deal with this sobering prospect later on in the context of our discussion of perishing (chapter 10). In the meantime, however, we suggest that our awareness of a still emerging cosmos makes room for human creativity beyond anything the human mind has ever met before. There may even be room for what is now referred to as "transhumanism," an extension of the universe's creativity beyond what evolution has produced so far. Provided this extension of human creativity preserves and expands the reign of goodness and is motivated by the virtues of hope, love, and humility, theology need not rule out the extension of our digital age's accelerating creativity and complexity into the production of new and unprecedented kinds of being. Research in genetics, nanotechnology, robotics, computer science, and the cognitive sciences is risky, and it could easily lead to monstrous outcomes. However, convergence supports this research as theologically significant at least in principle. Human technology has the potential to contribute positively to the ongoing creation of the universe.

Fourth, the scientific quest for beginnings that led to Big Bang cosmology is of interest to convergence because it coincides with the nearly *universal human search for origins*. Although we appreciate contrast's distinction between creation theology and Big Bang theory, the passionate religious concern for origins cannot be completely disentangled from the contemporary scientist's quest for initial cosmic causes and conditions. Much of the energy motivating scientific inquiry about our earliest cosmic roots stems from the persistently mythic orientation of human consciousness. A scientist's sense of wonder about cosmic origins is not entirely separable from the perennial human need to have a story of how things were in the beginning and how things got to be the way they are now. Cosmologists, geologists, and biologists should be honest enough to admit how much they share personally with ancient mythic and religious concern about origins. Even though Big Bang theory is conceptually and theologically distinguishable from the religious quest for origins, the two are existentially inseparable. The two quests may diverge as they unfold in their distinct spheres of understanding, but they both stem from a common human longing to discover where we came from and where we are going. Human beings are forever intrigued by the question of origins and destiny even when they have formally rejected religious mythology and symbols.

Allow us to conclude our discussion of science and the doctrine of creation with one additional suggestion. Convergence observes that the creation faith of Jews, Muslims, and Christians is not only consistent with, but also supportive of, the whole adventure of modern scientific inquiry. Before the rise of modern science, the theological doctrine of creation had for centuries already suffused the Western mind with a sense that the world is a contingent creation of God. To say that the world is "contingent" is to say that it need not have existed at all. Obviously the world exists, but to people of faith it is dependent on God's goodness for both its existence and its specific characteristics. This theological understanding of a contingent universe, we propose, gives a stature to empirical inquiry and scientific method that the ancient idea of an eternal, uncreated world does not.[12]

To understand this puzzling suggestion, let us suppose for a moment that the universe was not created and that it "simply exists." Until recently many philosophers believed that the world exists necessarily. Even Einstein, as we have seen, was of this opinion, at least for a while. However, if the universe exists eternally and necessarily, it has no choice as to what kind of universe it must be. If it exists necessarily, as the philosopher Baruch Spinoza, Einstein's intellectual hero, insisted, the universe could never have been other than what it is.

If that were the case, however, the empirical imperative that gives rise to modern science—namely, that we need to *look at* the universe before trying to understand it—would be irrelevant. For if the universe were necessary, we could simply sit at our desks and logically deduce its every feature, at least in principle. Empirical observation and fieldwork would be unnecessary. Thinkers of the past who believed the universe has existed forever would find it strange that we actually have to look at the world to understand it. For example, in the early seventeenth century, when Galileo was looking at the heavens through his new telescope, some contemporary Aristotelian philosophers refused to take his observations seriously. Physics, they thought, is purely theoretical rather than experimental.

However, if the universe is the free creation of God, as creation faith implies, this means that there is no necessity for its existing at all. Likewise there is no necessity for its being the kind of universe it is. So we cannot understand the natural world through pure deduction. We have to leave our cubicles and go out and *experience* it. That is, we have to examine it empirically, in the manner of modern science.

Our point then is that the Abrahamic faiths, unlike much ancient and modern materialist philosophy, are distinctive in believing that the natural world and its characteristics are the consequence of a completely free decision on the part of a creator God. This faith perspective, convergence suggests, allows us to be surprised by the facts we find as we investigate the world. It is within an intellectual and cultural milieu shaped by Abrahamic creation faith, therefore, that empirical method and scientific inquiry have blossomed and flourished. Science owes much more to faith and theology than most intellectuals today have noticed.

CHAPTER 6

Can Chemistry Alone Explain Life?

CONFLICT

Yes. Life is reducible to chemical elements and purely physical processes. This is the only answer science allows to this chapter's question. No matter how mysterious it initially appears to be, any reality we encounter, including complex living organisms, can eventually be broken down into material units governed by blind physical laws. Life is reducible to chemical processes, and chemistry in turn is reducible to physics. If you oppose this assumption, you will only be standing in the way of scientific progress. If you leave even the slightest opening for mysterious, nonphysical "explanations" of life, you are an enemy of truth.

Sometimes people call our point of view "reductionism," and most of us who follow the conflict approach to science and faith are happy to accept that label even though there is room for different interpretations of it. In any case, as Francis Crick correctly puts it, reductionism is "largely responsible for the spectacular developments of modern science."[1] Who, you may ask, is Francis Crick? He is the renowned twentieth-century scientist who, together with James Watson, discovered the double helix formation of DNA and thus revolutionized our whole understanding of life. With the help of many other scientists, he demonstrated conclusively that life has a purely physical and chemical basis. The DNA molecule in the nucleus of eukaryotic cells determines the shape and characteristics of the resultant organism. And DNA, you must remind yourself, is just a chain of atoms. "The ultimate aim of the modern movement in biology," Crick says, "is to explain all of life in terms of chemistry and physics."[2] This is as clear a formulation of our reductionist program as you will ever find.

Our job then is to stop at nothing in the effort to explain things physically and chemically, that is, without resorting to mysticism. We are scientific naturalists, so no territory is off limits to scientific probing. We believe that science is able to provide a purely materialist and atomistic explanation not only of life, but also of intelligence, ethics, and religion. Our objective, in other words, is to "demystify" the universe completely. Any recourse to the idea of God in the explanation of life is especially at odds with the advance of scientific knowledge. Consequently, we are forced once again to conclude that faith conflicts with science.

Our reductionist ideals are not unprecedented. Many centuries ago the pre-Socratic Greek philosopher Democritus (ca. 460–370 BCE) declared that "atoms" and "the void" are the sole constituents of everything real. His materialist atomism still strikes us as powerfully explanatory. Atomistic explanation of the universe seems so completely right to us that we find it intellectually irresistible. Our goal then is to remove any sense that life is an impenetrable mystery. Of course, during the evolution of life more and more complex beings have gradually emerged, but they are not the creation of God. They are all reducible, in the final analysis, to lifeless chemical elements and impersonal physical processes understandable in terms of mathematics.

There is no room left, therefore, for vitalism. Vitalism is the belief that a mysterious nonphysical force is necessary to transform lifeless matter into living organisms. There are still a few vitalists around, but their number is diminishing every day in the face of more refined chemical and physical analysis. Not only vitalism but also the whole world of faith and theology has been rendered completely superfluous by our discovery of the purely physical basis of life.

Today, no doubt, physics has shown that the material elements to which life is reducible are much more subtle than ancient atomists and modern materialists have supposed. Nonetheless, educated people realize now that materialist reductionism—or, if you prefer, "physicalism"—is the only legitimate approach to understanding living phenomena. The push toward reductionism in science has been gathering momentum ever since the seventeenth century. The science of Galileo, Descartes, and Newton began the process of transforming the whole universe into physical particles and mechanisms. Science didn't get off the ground until early modern thinkers began to expel occult "forces" and supernatural agency from their ideas about the natural world. Science today therefore must continue to erase every trace of mysticism from our understanding of life.

In the nineteenth century, physicists added credibility to the battle against vitalism by formulating the laws of thermodynamics. These are the laws that have to do with the transformation and conservation of energy. The well-known Second Law of Thermodynamics implies that the universe is running down energetically, drifting irreversibly from order to disorder, until eventually all life and consciousness will be dissolved into a state of final lifelessness and mindlessness. This running down is known as "entropy." It implies clearly that life is reducible to nonliving stuff not only in principle but also eventually in fact. Vitalists claim that the complex organization of matter in cells and organisms is evidence of a life force that contradicts nature's overall entropic movement toward physical disorder. However, good scientists now realize that life is an expression, not a violation, of the Second Law.[3] Every trend in evolution toward more physical complexity is paid for energetically by a total net loss of order in the physical environment as a whole. The laws of physics and chemistry remain inviolable, and they are sufficient to explain the existence and attributes of all living beings.

Also in the nineteenth century our reductionist program gained its most important victory with the arrival of Darwin's evolutionary theory. Evolutionary biology presents us with the picture of living complexity emerging gradually out of inanimate matter over an immensity of time. The historical arrival of life lies on an unbroken continuum with lifeless molecular and atomic reality. There are no sharp breaks in the process of nature's unfolding. Then in the twentieth century, Crick, Watson, and others conclusively reduced life to material processes. Biochemical and molecular analysis of genes and living cells has shown that the "secret" of life lies not in anything spiritual or divine but in the makeup of nucleic and amino acids. No hidden mysteries or explanatory gaps remain for theology to occupy. No foothold remains for faith's fruitless speculations.

Recently, we must admit, science has become impressed with the marvelous self-organizing features of matter. Matter, we now realize, can spontaneously organize itself—using only a few simple computational principles—into enormously complex emergent structures, including cells, brains, and societies. Theology claims that something extraneous to matter, some mystical force or vitalistic impulse, is required to lift matter toward new instances of organized complexity. But we now see that physical reality has a completely natural tendency to self-organize. Some of us are open to the idea that with the appearance of life in evolution an ingredient known as "information" entered into the universe. But information is a purely natural ingredient of life. No supernatural impetus or intervention is required to impel lifeless matter toward creative new arrangements. Matter's own marvelous spontaneity and creativity, along with the idea of information, makes any appeal to the idea of God more superfluous than ever.

Finally, our reductionism will also allow us eventually to account for the *origin* of life chemically and physically. Although the specifics of this unintended occurrence still elude complete scientific comprehension, there can be no doubt that life's debut was a purely natural set of events.

CONTRAST

At first sight, the case for reductionism has some cogency. It has seduced many smart people into thinking about nature in an incredibly simplistic way. The clarity and economy of reductionist explanation appeals to a deeply human urge to find the simplest possible explanation for complex phenomena. As far as our understanding of life is concerned, the real "conflict" is not between science and faith but between reductionist materialism on the one hand and faith's sense of the irreducibility of life's mystery on the other.

Contrast accepts all established scientific discoveries, but it firmly rejects reductionism. Contrast, furthermore, is not opposed to chemical and physical analysis. Science rightly approaches things analytically, breaking complex things down into simpler components. Reductionism is the belief that analysis *alone* can lead to adequate understanding of living beings. It is an unscientific belief added on to science. The key to understanding reductionism is to notice its use of terms such as only, exclusively, merely, or nothing but, as, for example, in its claim that life is merely or nothing but chemistry. Reductionists are people who believe that the *only* appropriate way to understand life and other complex things is to break them down into their subordinate particulars. Contrast rejects this belief and instead allows for many ways of understanding life.

Reductionism is another aspect of the beliefs we identified earlier as scientism, scientific naturalism, and materialism. As such, reductionism is not science but part of the naturalistic belief system. Along with the scientism that underlies it, reductionism provides an overarching, unbending framework—indeed a worldview—for trying to make sense of the complex universe in as simple a way as possible. Contrast agrees that chemical analysis is *one* way of understanding life, but not the only way. It allows that there are other avenues to understanding life as well, including theology. These additional ways of explaining do not compete with, but instead complement, chemical and physical analysis. Contrast, in other words, endorses explanatory pluralism. It assumes that multiple levels of explanation are necessary to understand anything at all. We refer to our approach as "layered explanation," and we define *reductionism* as the suppression of layered explanation. Let us explain.

By "layered explanation," we mean that everything in our experience is subject to more than one level of understanding and that the distinct levels need not compete with or contradict one another. Take, for example, the page you are reading right now. At how many levels can you explain why this page exists? Here are at least three:

Level 1: This page exists because a printing press stamped letters in black ink on white paper.

Level 2: This page exists because the book's author is trying to summarize for you the contrast approach to the question of whether life is reducible to chemistry.

Level 3: This page exists because Paulist Press invited the book's author to write an introductory work on science's relationship to faith.

Notice that these three explanations do not compete with one another. You can accept all three levels without fear that they are mutually contradictory. It would be nonsense to claim, for example, that this page exists merely because of a printing press *rather than* because an author is trying to get some ideas across. Likewise, it would be foolish to maintain that this page exists only because of a publisher's wish to have a new book on science and faith *rather than* because a printing press has stamped ink on this page. All three layers (and more) are essential to understanding why this page exists, and they don't conflict with one another.

Analogously, to maintain that chemical processes explain the existence of cells and organisms does not logically conflict with the belief that life exists because of God's infinite love and generosity. To claim with Crick that the secret to the existence of a living cell lies in chemistry alone is like saying that a printing press *rather than* an author's ideas accounts for the page you are reading. Layered explanation means that different levels of explanation may coexist without mutual tension or opposition. Your discovery, for instance, that a printing press caused words and sentences to appear on this page in no way diminishes the causal role of Paulist Press in producing the book on which this page appears. Likewise, science's discovery that chemical analysis explains the existence of life in no way rules out divine creativity at another level of explanation.

Our insistence on layered explanation applies as well to evolutionary accounts of life. Evolution has a lot to say about life, but when the evolutionary naturalist declares that natural selection *rather than* God accounts for living diversity, this is parallel to making the illogical claim that the page you are reading can be adequately explained by the chemistry of ink and paper *rather than* by the author's ideas or the publisher's initiative.

This page, contrast agrees, exists because of the chemical properties that allow black ink to bond with white paper. But this is only one of several levels of explanation. Acknowledging the causal role of a printing press or the bonding properties of black ink and white paper does not rule out the operative presence of deeper explanatory levels as well, such as the publisher's initiative and the author's efforts to have you understand the relationship of science to theology. These deeper causal levels, of course, are completely hidden from any chemical analysis of this page, but they are clearly essential to an adequate understanding of why this page exists. Likewise, God's love and generosity will not show up in a laboratory's analysis of the chemistry of life, but this does not mean that divine influence has nothing to do with the existence of life.

Unlike vitalism (at least as materialists understand it), our contrast approach does not look for divine influence in the gaps of life's chemical makeup. We refuse to place theology in a competitive relationship with chemical and physical accounts of life. In layered explanation each level of understanding is logically distinct from the others and cannot be mapped onto or reduced to the others. For example, the publisher's intention to make this book available to you will not show up while you are in the process of examining the mechanical operation of the printing press or while you are analyzing the chemistry of ink and paper. Similarly, if you are a biochemist you should not expect to discover divine causation at the level of your chemical analysis of life. And if you are an evolutionary biologist you should not make arbitrary reductionist claims that natural selection is the *only* permissible way to make sense of living diversity. Nor should representatives of conflict smugly conclude that they have debunked faith's conviction that God is the author of life simply because they have come across no spectator evidence of direct divine manipulation at the level of cellular or evolutionary biology.

If an examination of the chemistry of ink and paper is as deep as you want to go in accounting for this page, you will never become aware of the deeper levels of causation that brought it about. However, if you take a layered approach to explanation you can reach a richer understanding of everything. If you are willing to take a layered approach to your understanding of life, for example, you will take into account causal factors that chemical analysis has to leave out. You may even make room for a theological understanding of life.

Finally, contrast insists that reductionism is too suffocating for the inquisitive human mind. Reductionism, that is, the suppression of layered explanation, makes the world too small for open-minded people. We believe that very little of the totality of things can ever fall subject to science's analytical control. Science can tell us much but not everything about life and other phenomena. What we object to is not analysis but the decree that no dimensions of reality are permitted to fall outside the reach of analytical science. Such a requirement is far too confining for the wide-ranging radar of the human mind. Human inquiry needs to be nourished by other ways of understanding, ways that do not contradict science but that are complementary to science. One of these sources of nourishment is theology.

Why, though, do so many scientific thinkers become reductionists? We cannot answer this question comprehensively here, but we suspect that one reason reductionism is so appealing is that it gives one an exhilarating, though illusory, sense of intellectual control over nature. Reductionism in other words unconsciously serves other interests than the humble desire to know. Humans, as our religions realistically instruct us, have always had a deadly inclination to subject the totality of reality to their own felt supremacy, whether politically, economically, militarily, or intellectually. Reductionists uncritically assume that scientific analysis is enough to satisfy the long human quest for cognitional command over the world. Consequently, they take theistic faith to be a rival to their reductionism rather than a completely distinct way of understanding life. Faith's grateful trust in the irreducible mystery of God that underlies all of life is a threat to the reductionist's appetite for intellectual dominion. For true reductionists the whole objective of science is to expel all vestiges of mystery from the cosmos.

Contrast, however, suggests that genuine science comes not from the will to power but from the humble desire to know. We object to reductionism because it is rooted not in the desire to know but in the will to power. In the quest to understand life, we applaud science's innocent method of looking into things to find out their chemical and physical structure. What we object to is the "single vision" that heartlessly reduces the inexhaustible mystery of life to the mundane state of "merely" lifeless matter.

CONVERGENCE

We agree with contrast that life requires multiple "layers" of understanding. Life may be understood, for example, at the levels of chemical analysis, evolutionary biology, and theological inquiry. We see difference but no contradiction in these diverse approaches. However, convergence is also interested in exploring how the various levels are related to one another. It is not enough just to point out that there are different levels of explanation. We want to see how they are connected.

We find the connection we are looking for by situating life in the context of the new cosmic story that forms the backbone of all our attempts in this book to relate science to theology. Instead of being content with a purely analytical understanding of the structure of living cells and organisms, we look for a "narrative coherence" that ties the history of life to the billions of years of lifeless physical and chemical processes that came into play long before the birth of life. Thus, for convergence the emergence of life is not only a chemical affair but also an important episode in a momentous cosmic drama. We are interested not only in the alphabet, lexicon, and grammar of the life story but also in its meaning.

Although the contrast point of view clarifies the difference between analytical science and theology, we prefer a much more dialogical approach. We are grateful for the hard work of scientific analysis, especially since it fills in our picture of the universe as a long and still unwinding journey. Breaking life down into elemental units in effect takes us back into the remote cosmic chapters of this itinerary. Analysis of atoms or cells in a contemporary laboratory setting gives us a picture of what the universe was like billions of years ago. Analytical science today is portraying ever more precisely the earliest stages of cosmic becoming that had previously eluded human understanding. For example, the massive CERN accelerator near Geneva, Switzerland, by decomposing atomic units today has the effect of allowing us to peer more closely than ever into the physical conditions during the first microseconds of our universe's existence. Likewise, expert analysis of cells and organisms takes us back in time to the earliest episodes in the odyssey of life. Apart from such contemporary scientific analysis we would have no sense of the narrative depth of nature and life in the universe.

Once again, however, a shift of metaphors from design to drama allows us to understand the natural world in a more comprehensive way than analysis alone permits. A narrative reading of life's atomic and molecular alphabet, we submit, allows us to see the relationship between chemistry and life in a way that is both scientifically and theologically illuminating. Old-fashioned reductionists such as Daniel Dennett view life mechanistically, as ultimately "nothing but" lifeless stuff into which cells can be chemically resolved. Convergence, however, looks at the universe narratively and not just reductively. From our perspective, the atomic and chemical layers that scientific analysis has exposed are *chapters* or *eras* in a long cosmic story and not just building blocks for cells and organisms. The subatomic, atomic, and molecular layers that analytical science uncovers in probing the physical architecture of life are also a historical record of the long staging process that led up to the dramatic debut of life.

However, analysis lays out distinct scenes in a drama whose depth of meaning we can arrive at only if we are willing to *wait* to see how it all turns out. The role of faith is to encourage us to wait for the meaning of the story of life to reveal itself. Abrahamic religions refuse to assume that we are ever in a privileged position here and now to decide whether things have a meaning, or what this meaning might be. Convergence, accordingly, suggests that natural science can never make us so sure of ourselves that we can simply declare that life is "merely" or "nothing but" chemistry. Unlike reductionism, our narrative sense of life leaves open the possibility that something truly momentous, though still beyond our present reach, is going on in the drama of life and the universe. Right now we are enmeshed in a yet unfinished story. The role of faith, with its motifs of promise and hope, is to keep our minds and hearts open to the possible disclosure of a new and deeper narrative coherence up ahead. Faith encourages us to remain open to surprise as the drama of life continues to play itself out.

What we look for in our understanding of life, therefore, is not analytical precision—important as this is—but narrative meaning. We look for the kind of satisfaction we anticipate when attending a play, watching a movie, or reading a novel. In such cases we are in search of a revelatory moment when all the previously unintelligible episodes come together and the drama begins to disclose its meaning. Similarly, since we are presently immersed in the ongoing drama of life we can have only an anticipatory, and hence vague, sense of its meaning. If the drama of life has a meaning or meanings, it is only on the horizon of the future that we can now look for these to emerge. Faith, by its encouragement to hope, has the indispensable function of pointing our minds in the direction of this future. Faith therefore is not a flight from understanding but, along with science, an essential component in the quest to understand what life is all about.

Convergence begins, as we have already said, with our new awareness that life is part of a cosmic drama still in the making. Scientific analysis cannot tell us what life is really all about. Convergence, moreover, recognizes that the mechanistic or architectural perspective with which reductionists approach cells and organisms can lead to the mistaken belief that life is merely chemistry. Our dramatic perspective, though, insists that the universe was never merely lifeless. The drama of life began not 3.8 billion years ago, but 13.7 billion years ago. The idea that nature is *essentially* lifeless is the product of a stagnant reductionism that fails to look broadly at the drama of nature.

Scientific analysis, as it breaks life down into nonliving components, in effect takes us back in time, in the direction of increasing "de-coherence." Scientific reduction discloses a remote cosmic past prior to life, long before the elements began to cluster into cellular form, before life's molecules had begun to form, all the way back to an epoch before even atoms of hydrogen and helium existed. Analysis leads the mind in the direction of the primordial dispersal or fragmentation of elemental entities. To find coherence, therefore, one has to abandon mere analysis. After taking the analytical scientific journey into the remote cosmic past, we must turn around, leaving the reductionists behind, and start following the cosmic itinerary as it moves in the direction of an ever-surprising future. We discover that in the long cosmic story, matter slowly moves from a relatively diffused state toward more complex kinds of coherence. As the early universe begins to cool, atoms come into existence and are eventually synthesized into increasingly complex molecules. Molecules are then taken up into living cells, and cells into increasingly complex organisms. Life emerges, and a surprising kind of coherence gradually takes the place of primordial de-coherence.

And so, after making our journey from the remote past we arrive once again in the present, but by now we have learned that the cosmic journey still goes on. Maybe we have recently emerged from what will turn out in the long run to be only the cosmic dawn. If there is a meaning to this story, however, it will be apprehended not by analysis of the past but by waiting in patient expectation to see how things turn out in life's long run. Faith orients our consciousness to hope for a not yet visible future. Faith invites us to anticipate that the whole cosmic story may reach an unimaginable climax up ahead. In the meantime, however, we can at least contemplate the fact that with the emergence of life something dramatically new has already entered into the cosmic story, something irreducible to chemistry.

Our commonsense intuition that life is not reducible to chemistry is implicit in the very fact that scientists and universities distinguish departments of biology from those of chemistry or physics. Biology exists as a distinct department in academic institutions only because human beings cannot help sensing a dramatic difference between life and nonlife. If life were really reducible to lifeless matter there would be only one department in every academic institution: physics.

However, whether we admit it explicitly or not, we intuitively understand that living beings possess certain dramatic qualities that only persons can grasp. We are tacitly aware that something about life clearly slips through the wide meshes of chemistry's net. This "something" is not a supernatural or vitalistic force. Rather it is life's capacity to *strive*. To be alive means to be able to strive and possibly *achieve* something.[4] Whether it is a microorganism searching for nourishment, a college sophomore craving academic success, or a middle-aged woman looking to find meaning in her life, striving (or at least the capacity to strive) is a distinguishing mark of life. Right now, for example, you are striving to make sense of this chapter. So you can experience immediately the fact that your own aliveness consists at least in part of making the effort to achieve something. Maybe you will succeed, or maybe not, but there can be no doubt that you can feel yourself at least striving.

Apart from the capacity to strive, you would not be alive, and it is your personal experience of striving that allows you to identify other beings as also alive and therefore as having a special kinship with you. You belong to an exceptional community, that of living beings. And it is their collective striving—along with their failures and achievements— that gives to the universe its specifically dramatic character.

Reductionist attempts to arrive at the secret of life leave out any appreciation of this dramatic factor of striving that allows us to talk about life at all. By insisting that life is reducible to physical and chemical processes, Crick and other hardcore reductionists overlook the defining factor that draws all living beings together, namely, their capacity to strive. Purely chemical processes do not strive. They passively obey deterministic laws. They have no capacity either to succeed or fail. Living beings, however, can succeed or fail because they first of all have the capacity to reach toward goals. Even the simplest instances of metabolism may not be "just chemistry." In the building of membranes to keep themselves from being reabsorbed into the nonliving environment, the simplest of cells may already be putting forth a kind of "effort" that is absent from purely chemical reactions.[5] Living organisms are plainly irreducible to nonliving chemical processes.

When convergence talks about the drama of life, therefore, it is thinking especially of living beings' struggling, failing, and succeeding in their common striving to achieve goals. There is no real drama apart from this striving. A purely physical or chemical analysis of life is blind to the dramatic aspect of life and the cosmos. No doubt the striving of living beings depends upon invariant physical and chemical processes at work within cells and organisms. However, physical or chemical analysis alone overlooks the drama of striving, struggling, achieving, and failing that goes on in the life world. Ironically, however, the passionate effort by reductionists such as Crick to break life down into lifeless units is itself an instance of personal *striving* that gives considerable drama to the scientific quest and to the reductionist's own personal life. Convergence firmly believes, however, that the entire modern reductionist enterprise of striving to reduce life to nonliving "matter" is itself a tragic failure in the history of human consciousness.[6]

This failure becomes obvious as soon as we take into account the element of *information* that the emergence of life has brought into the universe. Nothing demonstrates the futility of analytical attempts to reduce life to chemistry more clearly than the informational ingredient that patterns physical reality into living cells and tissue. Life, we have now come to see, is not just matter plus energy. Life is matter plus energy plus information.[7]

The evidence that life is more than chemistry lies in the arrangement of "letters" in the DNA of living cells. The informational aspect in cells consists of the *specific sequence* of DNA's four letters (A, T, G, and C). Chemical analysis cannot tell us why the letters are arranged in this or that specific order. The chemical factors that bind atoms together in DNA function in the same way in all living cells, but the specific sequence of letters in DNA is not determined by chemical processes. The informational arrangement of letters in the genetic code is what makes one organism turn out to be a human being, another a monkey, and another a snake. This informational difference is enough to show that life is more than "just chemistry."[8]

In order to notice the informational dimension of life, however, you have to move up to another reading level distinct from that of chemical analysis. Viewed analytically, DNA is "just chemistry," but from an informational point of view the specific sequence of nucleotides is the most important aspect of the cell. This sequence is logically distinguishable from the chemical routines going on in all living beings. We are not suggesting here that an invisible divine hand directly manipulates the "letters" in the DNA. And we are not defending some version of intelligent design. Rather we are simply pointing out that both the informational aspect of life and the element of striving make life irreducible to chemical processes.

With the arrival of information and striving, the cosmic story undergoes a dramatic transformation. The introduction of information and striving (and later intelligence) happens so unobtrusively that a purely reductionist perspective doesn't even notice it. No physical or chemical laws are violated. Nevertheless, without disturbing any physical, chemical, or biological routines, meaning and purpose can enter into the drama of life without ever showing up on science's analytical registers.

CHAPTER 7

Can Science Explain Intelligence?

CONFLICT

Yes. Science has shown that your mind is a purely natural outcome of the evolution of life on Earth. Since God does not exist, we are required to look for purely natural explanations of everything, including the human mind. Your intelligence, especially your abstract thinking, may seem completely different from everything else going on in the physical universe, but objective scientific research now shows that your mind is reducible to your brain. If your brain stops working, your mind does too. It follows therefore that your mental activity is a product of your brain and nothing else.

During the past half-century science has made considerable progress in understanding the brain. Even though your brain and nervous system are exceedingly complex, they are composed of atoms and molecules. Moreover, recent advances in the cognitive sciences are now helping us understand the "wiring" of the brain as well as the computational structure of mental operations. Just as your computer requires no spiritual components to produce its amazing output, so also the functioning of your brain is enough to produce thought. Purely physical analysis can explain your mind and its aptitudes, at least in principle if not yet in fact.

Conflict's commitment to materialist explanation has grown increasingly confident as science continues to expose the tight connection between mind and brain.[1] So it is time for you, the reader, to realize that your own mind is a purely physical network of tissue and to accept the implications of that judgment. Listen to philosopher Daniel Dennett as he spells out bluntly what science implies about the mind:

> There is only one sort of stuff, namely matter–the physical stuff of physics, chemistry, and physiology—and the mind is somehow nothing but a physical phenomenon. In short, the mind is the brain. According to the materialists we can (in principle!) account for every mental phenomenon using the same physical principles, laws and raw materials that suffice to explain radioactivity, continental drift, photosynthesis, reproduction, nutrition and growth.[2]

Francis Crick, whom we introduced in the previous chapter, echoes Dennett's materialism. Presenting us with what he calls his "Astonishing Hypothesis," he writes, "You, all your joys and your sorrows, your memories and your ambitions, your sense of identity and free will, are in fact no more than the behavior of a vast assembly of nerve cells and their associated molecules."[3] The prescientific religious belief that you have an immortal soul, that you are cared for by God, and that you are special among living beings is no longer tenable. As Crick goes on to say, "Scientific certainty (with all its limitations) can in the long run rid us of the superstitions of our ancestors."[4]

Theological traditions picture the universe as a hierarchy of distinct levels of being, each graded according to its unique degree of importance relative to God. Matter, in this now obsolete worldview, is the lowest level and the least important. Plants, since they are alive, are more significant than mere matter; animals are more valuable than plants; and humans are more significant than animals. Then, at the highest level of the hierarchy, traditional theologies typically locate God. As we move up this hierarchy, each level is said to exhibit features that are lacking in those beneath it. Theology ignorantly decrees that there is an "ontological discontinuity" as we pass from one level up to the next. It naïvely teaches people of faith that the "higher" levels cannot be understood in terms of the levels beneath them.[5]

Today, however, science has destroyed this ancient hierarchical view of the universe. As Crick points out, the majority of neuroscientists "believe that the idea of the soul is a myth,"[6] and they deny that mind somehow exists independently of a material brain. To conflict the classical theological hierarchy is mere mystification that stands in the way of scientific progress. By denying that mind is purely physical, theology has placed arbitrary limits on what science can discover or explain on its own. Even though some version of the hierarchical vision has shaped the consciousness of most people on our planet for thousands of years, science now shows that theological "top-down" explanation of mind is hopelessly out of date. We are now confident that science can explain not only life, but also human consciousness from the "bottom up," that is, in terms of chemistry and other "lower-level" sciences. We no longer think of mind as more real than matter.

Mind, let's face it, is a product of evolution. The *ultimate* explanation of your mental life lies in the blind, impersonal process of natural selection. You are intelligent because you have inherited a certain kind of brain from your ancestors. You may be proud of the problem-solving capacities of your mind, but you should thank the evolutionary process—going back more than 2 million years—for sculpting the specialized kind of brain you have inherited from your early human ancestors. Only those adaptive ancestral brains that happened to have the cognitive skills to survive the hazards of life during the Pleistocene period survived long enough to pass on their genes to future generations, including our own.

The natural history leading to your brain and mind, you must never forget, was itself mindless. Even though evolution has recently produced intelligent human subjects, the physical processes that brought minds into existence are essentially devoid of intelligence. Duke University philosopher Owen Flanagan insightfully points out that even though human intelligence is a marvelous evolutionary product, biology now "demonstrates how intelligence arose from totally insensate origins."[7] Dennett agrees: "The designs in nature [including intelligent beings] are nothing short of brilliant, but the process of design that generates them is utterly lacking in intelligence of its own."[8] Darwin's science now offers the deepest available explanation of all manifestations of life, including human intelligence.

This means that theology can have no illuminating role to play along-side of biology and chemistry in contemporary attempts to understand human intelligence.

CONTRAST

We commented on materialist reductionism in the previous chapter. What we said there about the irreducibility of life to chemistry applies also to the incoherent attempts by scientism to reduce mind to purely physical processes. Here we confine our comments to conflict's claim that mind can be explained ultimately as an evolutionary adaptation. Is this a reasonable claim? We think not. In its attempt to explain mind as "ultimately" a product of natural selection, evolutionary naturalism shows itself to be a logically self-subverting and hence groundless set of beliefs.

Before stating why we consider evolutionary naturalism illogical, however, we want to emphasize that contrast fully accepts the scientific information that underlies Darwinian evolutionary theory. As we insisted earlier, we object not to evolutionary science but to evolutionary naturalism. In the present chapter we reject the *belief* that evolutionary biology can provide an adequate or ultimate explanation of human intelligence. In their Darwinian "explanation" of mind, evolutionary naturalists logically undermine any confidence we (or they) might have that their minds can put us in touch with truth.

How so? Evolutionary naturalists claim that the natural process that produced minds—including, of course, their own—is essentially mindless. Is it reasonable to claim that mindlessness can be the final explanation of mind? Maybe you, the reader, can answer this question for yourself. Assume, for the time being, that you are Dawkins, Dennett, Flanagan, or some other evolutionary naturalist. That is, suppose you are convinced that the ultimate explanation of your own mind and all its operations is the brute, dumb, silent world of mind-less physical processes, including natural selection. Then if the entire causal series that produced your intelligence is at bottom unintelligent, as Flanagan claims, why should you *trust* that your mind can make any truthful claims at all here and now? Doesn't your evolutionary naturalism sabotage any reason you might have for trusting your own mind's performance? Shouldn't simple logic and intellectual honesty lead you to conclude that if evolutionary naturalism is true, there is no reason for you to trust your mind?

We are not alone in raising this question. Charles Darwin also wondered whether we can be confident about our claims if they are the outcome of a purely mindless process of natural selection. He wrote:

> With me the horrid doubt always arises whether the convictions of man's mind, which has been developed from the mind of the lower animals, are of any value or at all trustworthy. Would any one trust in the convictions of a monkey's mind, if there are any convictions in such a mind?[9]

Similarly, the late highly esteemed philosopher Richard Rorty, no friend of theology, rightly remarked:

> The idea that one species of organism is, unlike all the others, oriented not just toward its own increased prosperity [that is, toward "fitness"] but toward Truth, is as un-Darwinian as the idea that every human being has a built-in moral compass—a conscience that swings free of both social history and individual luck.[10]

Neither Rorty nor Darwin, however, seems to have grasped the gravity of his suspicions. Each of them, if asked, would claim to be a lover of truth, and each of these highly intelligent thinkers manifestly trusts his own mind as it makes the claims we have just quoted. However, a purely Darwinian account of intelligence, though it may tell a reliable story of how human minds arose gradually, cannot by itself *justify* the trust underlying its own intellectual performance. Indeed, evolutionary naturalism (as distinct from evolutionary biology) logically undermines any trust that the mind can lead one to truth. Dennett, Flanagan, and other materialists tell you that the conflict approach is right and the contrast approach is wrong. But given their belief that mindlessness is the ultimate explanation of their own minds, why should you pay any attention to their claims? What is there in their account of human intelligence that should lead you or them to trust their minds?[11]

Evolutionary naturalism's account of intelligence seems more like alchemy than science. It asks you to believe that a totally dumb set of physical processes can transform the dross of mindless matter into the lustrous gold of intelligence. But it never tells you exactly how this occurs. It simply recites the formula that small accidental changes over an enormously long period of time are enough to accomplish this miraculous transformation. But there is nothing in a purely chemical or evolutionary account of your mind that can tell you why you should trust it. To be sure, chemical and evolutionary factors are necessary to the emergence of your mind, and contrast encourages scientific study of the natural history that led to the evolutionary invention of brains. But a purely physical or evolutionary account is not enough to explain why, here and now, you may justifiably *trust* your mind.

If the question is, How did intelligence emerge in evolution?, then science can provide important details concerning its origin and development. But if the question is, Why do you trust your mind?, some other explanatory ingredient is needed. The fact is, of course, that you do at least tacitly *believe* your mind is trustworthy. If you didn't believe this you wouldn't even be reading this chapter. If you didn't already trust your mind's capacity for correct understanding you wouldn't be raising the questions you are asking right now about whether our contrast approach is right or wrong. Clearly, then, you do trust your mind to arrive at intelligibility and truth. But how, if the evolutionary naturalists are right, can you justify this trust?

Theology, we think, can provide what is missing here, and it can do so in a way that does not compete or conflict with scientific accounts. Contrast, you will recall, endorses "layered explanation" because everything is open to a plurality of noncompeting accounts. Layered explanation in the context of this chapter means that you can understand your own intelligence in both scientific and theological ways without contradiction.

To make our point as clearly as possible let us begin with a question: Why is your mind working at this moment as you are reading this chapter? How many ways can you answer this question? At one level you may answer that your mind is working because your brain's neurons are firing and synaptic connections are being activated, and so on. Neuroscience elaborates on this kind of answer in an extraordinarily nuanced way, and contrast encourages neuroscientists to take their own physical understanding of the brain and mind as far as they can. Likewise, contrast encourages evolutionary biologists to explore the fascinating history of genetic transmission that has led to the emergence of your capacity for thought.

However, even though science can explain in physical, neurological, and evolutionary terms why you are thinking, it cannot cover everything that goes into the making of a mind. One of the conditions essential for the emergence of mind in evolution is that the universe in which minds evolve be intelligible. If the universe were inherently unintelligible, there could be no intelligent activity at all, and hence no minds.

Science, however, cannot tell you why the universe is intelligible. Nor can science tell you why truth is worth seeking or why you may trust your mind. And yet you need to *believe* these three things or else your thought processes couldn't even get off the ground. Maybe you have never noticed it before, but your thinking requires believing. You have to believe that the world is intelligible, that truth is worth seeking, and that your mind can be trusted to lead you to understanding and truth. So any *full* explanation of why you are thinking at the moment has to answer these three questions: Why is the universe intelligible? Why is truth worth seeking? Why can you trust your mind?

Science cannot help you here, since scientists too have to *believe* or trust that the universe is intelligible before they can even get started on their own quest for understanding. Yet theology can give you a reasonable answer to the three questions. The universe is intelligible ultimately because it is grounded in an infinite intelligence. Seeking the truth is a worthwhile endeavor ultimately because only the union of your mind with what is most real can bring real happiness and set you free from illusions. And you may trust your mind since it is already in the grasp of infinite meaning and truth. Before your mind can even ask a question, it has already tacitly surrendered to the allure of what is inexhaustibly intelligible and real. This is why you may justifiably trust your mind. By anticipating meaning and truth, your mind is already in the grasp of the infinite. By reducing your mind to mindless matter, evolutionary naturalism can only lead you to distrust your mind, whereas a theological worldview can fully justify your cognitional confidence. And it can do so without in any way conflicting with good science, including evolutionary biology.[12]

CONVERGENCE

The awakening of consciousness in human beings is the most important chapter of the cosmic drama so far. In human beings the universe has at last become conscious of itself. Recent discoveries in the fields of astronomy and cosmology, as well as biology, have now located human intelligence squarely *within* the cosmic story. Unlike conflict and contrast, convergence situates your mind within the narrative marrow of a universe that is still in the making. Science has now shown that beings endowed with a capacity for inquiry have come into existence from a universe estimated to be around 14 billion years old. Judging from all that the physical sciences have discovered, your mind belongs to an unfinished cosmos. It is not an alien intruder from another world. The truly interesting question, then, is not whether science can explain intelligence. To convergence the more important question is, What does it *mean* that the universe has now become conscious of itself?

Astrophysics and cosmology have led scientists to the realization that the existence of human consciousness entails a very specific kind of universe, one that possesses just the right physical characteristics to allow for the recent emergence of thought. Thus the question of whether science can explain intelligence now merges with the larger question of whether science can explain why our universe happens to be a mind-bearing one in the first place.

Astrophysicists have now concluded that the Big Bang universe has been pregnant with life and mind from its very inception 14 billion years ago. Obsolete materialist or "physicalist" worldviews regard the universe as essentially mindless, but now most scientists suspect that mind has emerged from a cosmos whose physical features are precisely such as to make the eventual existence of thought highly probable from the outset. During the earliest cosmic moments, mind was already starting to stir. Billions of years later it began to awaken. Now we wonder what kind and degree of consciousness the universe will have attained millions of years from now.

At any rate, the relatively recent debut of conscious self-awareness in evolution is evidence of an immense *cosmic* awakening. This dramatic occurrence alone should shock us into having new thoughts about the mind, the universe, and God. The entry of mind into the universe may seem unimpressive from the perspective of physics, chemistry, and evolutionary biology. After all, no laws of physics, chemistry, and biology were violated when mind emerged from the mud. From our narrative cosmic perspective, however, everything in nature looks different once we take mind into account. The recent emergence of conscious self-awareness—along with moral awareness, aesthetic sensitivity, and religious longing—is the most dramatic development ever to have occurred in the long cosmic adventure.

This is why, once again, convergence invites you to look at scientific discoveries and the meaning of faith panoramically and narratively. If you can learn to view the emergence of mind as part of a drama of cosmic becoming, the birth of "thought" will no longer seem to be the trivial occurrence that radical reductionists take it to be. With the coming of human thought the universe reveals potentialities and promises whose first seeds were sown many billions of years ago.

No doubt, Peter Atkins of Oxford University, a self-avowed materialist, will persist in his claim that everything in nature, including mind, is just physical "simplicity masquerading as complexity." Alex Rosenberg of Duke University, a devout advocate of reductionism, will still keep telling his students that it's all just protons, electrons, leptons, and suchlike. Jerry Coyne of the University of Chicago, whose faith in evolutionary naturalism has no limits, will continue to remind us that the high degree of accident and blind necessity in biological evolution renders the emergence of mind nothing but a fluke of nature. (Why he puts so much trust in his own mind, therefore, remains a mystery.) And Steven Weinberg of the University of Texas, our paragon of cosmic pessimism, will keep telling us that physics shows no trace of God or ultimate meaning.[13]

Not one of these servants of scientism even sees, let alone tries to make sense of the *story* of cosmic awakening that is going on beneath his feet. Each one values his mind way out of proportion to what his materialist worldview logically permits. Each fails to acknowledge that the mind he relies on so unquestioningly is a consequence of the most dramatic chapter ever to have occurred in cosmic history.

Convergence, for its part, finds in the drama of cosmic awakening a fertile new framework for understanding the relationship of science to faith. Our narrative perspective asks you to postpone making claims about whether and how science contradicts faith until you have looked at every new scientific discovery in terms of how it contributes to the shaping of our new sense of a cosmic story. Each distinct field of science understandably focuses on a relatively narrow range of data and leaves out any concern about the wider vision that we are recommending here. We do not object to the fact that scientists analyze and specialize, of course. What we object to is the fact that analysts and specialists sometimes generalize too soon and too narrowly.[14] We protest their attempts to unify all knowledge in terms of the limited concepts used in their own disciplines.[15] Specialization is necessary, but after looking at nature with the microscope, telescope, and the instrumentality of mathematics, we need to back up and take everything in from a narrative perspective.

Biology's inability to encompass methodologically the much broader cosmological context of human emergence has led many contemporary scientists and philosophers to the lazy and dubious conclusion that mind is "just" chemistry or "just" an evolutionary fluke. Mind, to the evolutionary materialist, is little more than an absurd and unintended outcome of random mutations and blind natural selection. But when we place the recent arrival of mind within the entire sweep of cosmic history, it takes on a dramatic significance that remains invisible from the specialized viewpoints of physics, chemistry, biology, and neuroscience.

Our convergence approach invites the reader to look at every scientific discovery in terms of a wider quest for narrative coherence. Rather than settle merely for mechanistic precision or mathematical certainty—both of which are laudatory goals—convergence situates scientific findings within the setting of a cosmic drama that may be read theologically as well. Full understanding of the cosmic story, we suggest, can be approached only through hopeful expectation and not through scientism's impatient demand for full analytical clarity in the here and now. Faith and theology prepare our minds to read the cosmic story at a different level of interest from that of scientific analysis. Because the narrative coherence we are looking for can be arrived at only in the future, it requires a posture of waiting and hoping. Whereas scientism looks to the cosmic past to understand nature, convergence looks to the cosmic future for a richer understanding of what is going on in the universe. Scientism takes an exclusively archeological, analytical approach that digs into the cosmic past to recover whatever fragments it can. Convergence, however, takes an *anticipatory* approach to understanding the still emerging universe.

Since the universe is still rising from the dust of its atomic past, it is not yet fully coherent or fully intelligible to our limited minds and methods of inquiry. The disposition of faith is that of encouraging us to look for deeper intelligibility up ahead. The hope enkindled by faith, therefore, is not illusory or escapist. Hope is not the same thing as naïve optimism. Rather it is the most realistic stance the mind can take as it surveys a universe that is still coming into being. If the universe is still being born, a hope directed toward what it may yet become is more supportive of the human mind's longing for understanding and truth than is the reductionist, backward-looking mentality that accompanies the myth of materialism.

To convergence, the universe provides at least a glimpse of its intelligibility in every new instance of matter and life. Nevertheless, in the recent emergence of mind the universe gives us more than a glimpse of its inner meaning. With the arrival of intelligence the universe gives birth to a kind of being whose vitality and happiness depend on its anticipation of the infinite: infinite being, meaning, truth, goodness, and beauty.

The universe has always been encompassed by the infinite, but in the emergence of conscious beings endowed with a "capacity for the infinite" the universe has made its most dramatic leap thus far. The universe has awakened not only into thought, but also into freedom. By giving rise to beings that have the potential for reflective self-awareness and hope, the universe demonstrates that it still has the reserve to become even *more* than it has been in the past. For this reason, only an anticipatory, hopeful cognitive stance can be fully proportionate to a world that is still in the process of becoming. Pure reductionism, in our perspective, is a refusal to face reality.

The fact that we humans can contribute in diverse ways to the process of the universe's becoming *more* implies also that we have a special standing within the whole of creation. As we shall see in chapter 10, our special dignity is already implied in the experience of ourselves as having a vocation to participate, each in a unique way, in the process of transformation that we call the universe. In our creativity, our capacity to form intimate relationships, our aspiration to act virtuously and to worship with others, we remain faithful to the cosmic story that has thrust us into existence. Our narrative, anticipatory perspective suggests that the meaning of our lives consists, at least in part, of our now taking a more deliberate role in the continuation of the cosmic drama.[16]

In an anticipatory way the cosmos, it now appears, was always enveloped by a potential to become subjective and conscious. Even when no intelligent subjects yet existed, the universe was already on a wide path that would eventually allow it to awaken into intelligence. The earliest chapters of the cosmic story were already seeded with the promise that mind—the capacity to grasp intelligibility and truth— would eventually come into the story. In our view the faith traditions that began in the Abrahamic hope for a new future fit comfortably within a cosmic story that, from its earliest moments, has held the promise of bursting eventually into thought, freedom, love, and the capacity to keep promises.

CHAPTER 8

Can We Be Good without God?

CONFLICT

Yes, indeed, at least if Darwin has anything to say about it. Evolutionary biology can now explain in a purely natural way why human beings are inclined to be moral. Morality, which means cooperating with and caring for others, is an evolutionary adaptation without which our species would never have survived and flourished. The tendency to cooperate allowed our ancestors to live long enough to reproduce and thus pass their cooperative genes on to future generations. We have inherited their adaptive genes. Our thesis, therefore, is that neither the origin nor the persistence of morality requires any theological explanation. We can be good without God and without faith. Morality, in other words, is a purely natural phenomenon.[1]

But if morality doesn't require faith in God, how is one to explain why we submit to moral imperatives at all? To be morally good, don't we need divine directives? No. Although older psychological and sociological explanations may still give reasonable responses to this question, today the best answer comes from Darwinian biology. Morality is merely the product of an impersonal evolutionary process *rather than* a free human response to an eternal goodness. Most humans are inclined to be moral not because an eternal divine law is stamped on their hearts, as theologians have claimed, but because evolution long ago began fashioning human organisms whose virtuous behavior increased the probability that their genes would survive into future generations. No doubt, cultural influences help determine the specific content of moral conduct, but the prohibition of uncooperative behavior is universal because it is built into our genes to be cooperative. In our opinion, natural selection, not theology, provides the *ultimate* explanation of the persistent imperative to live cooperatively with others.

Nowadays many evolutionists argue that "natural selection" applies more accurately to populations of genes shared by members of a species than to individual organisms.[2] We are moral beings because living cooperatively has contributed to human gene transmission and survival. Consequently, there is simply no need to explain or justify morality theologically.[3] According to the main religious traditions, selfless love of others is the high point of moral existence. Theologians have always claimed that the exercise of selfless love is impossible without the help of God. But evolutionists today trace the origin of virtue to unintended, accidental genetic occurrences that programmed some of our ancestors to be more cooperative and self-sacrificing than others. Ancestral groups in which genes for generous behavior were spread around sufficiently had a better chance of surviving and reproducing than those not so enriched. Gene survival, not God, is the ultimate source of even our noblest moral instincts.

Selfless regard for others is often called "altruism," and until recently the term was used primarily to characterize human virtue. However, today biologists point out that altruism emerged at least faintly much earlier in evolution than humans did. Altruism is already present in the mutual cooperation observable, for example, in ant colonies. Technically altruism in evolutionary biology involves putting one's own genetic future at risk for the sake of the survival of the larger population of genes one shares with one's kin. For example, in ant colonies the "workers" will not pass on their own genes because they are sterile, but their selfless behavior contributes to the survival of the whole colony and thus to what some biologists call "inclusive fitness." "A single ant or honey bee," the evolutionist Matt Ridley notes, "is as feeble and doomed as a severed finger. Attached to its colony, though, it is as useful as a thumb. It serves the greater good of its colony, sacrificing its reproduction and risking its life on behalf of the colony."[4]

Instances of this kind of altruism abound in the animal kingdom. Cooperation is a purely natural evolutionary development. So if ants can be dutiful without God, why can't we? Even our purest moral ideals have not descended from on high. Instead they simply radiate from the human genome. People of faith are deluded when they claim that moral imperatives have their origin in the mind or will of a divine lawgiver. The illusion of divine sanction may give codes of conduct a fictitious authority, but Darwinian science has exposed human morality as a purely natural outcome of our genes' need for immortality. It may *seem* that when we are virtuous we are motivated by eternal values, but Darwinians know better. It is not God, but genes, that are orchestrating the entire drama of ethical existence.

We realize that many readers who have followed the conflict approach so far will be skeptical of this thesis. So allow us to develop our Darwinian account of morality in a bit more detail. In the struggle for existence, according to Darwin, some organisms win and others lose. Those that win are called "fit" in the sense that they have a higher probability of surviving and reproducing than the losers. In the struggle to exist and reproduce, life involves competition, and the winners in the contest are those that adapt to their environments long enough to bear offspring. Still, no species can survive on competition alone. If a species is to endure for many generations, in addition to competing with others for the resources to sustain life, individuals must also coöperate with other members and even at times with other species. Evolution entails cooperation no less than competition. It even requires self-sacrifice.

As noted previously, when an organism sacrifices its own reproductive opportunities for the sake of preserving its family, group, or species, biologists call it "altruism." And, as we have already noted, in the case of human social existence, altruism and self-sacrifice are generally considered the highest expressions of morality. However, from an evolutionary point of view human virtue has its origin in the cooperation and altruism that already show up in prehuman forms of life. The genealogy of human morality may be traced all the way back into the process of gene transmission that goes on in the long story of life.

Darwin himself knew nothing about genes, and he thought of evolutionary selection as taking place primarily at the level of individual organisms. But now some highly respected evolutionists have concluded that natural selection applies more precisely to arrays of genes shared by many members of a species than to individual organisms alone. Thinking of selection in terms of populations of genes makes evolution statistically measurable, thus satisfying the quantitative interests of science. Evolutionary fitness still means the probability of reproductive success, but such success is not so much a property of individual organisms as of large groupings of genes. As long as a sufficient number of cooperative genes are present overall, a species has a relatively strong probability of surviving even if some individuals perish before having the opportunity to reproduce. So it is not necessarily the fittest individual organisms that will survive, but instead the fittest sets of genes.[5]

Suppose, for example, that a young prairie dog possesses genes that direct it to be more altruistic than its siblings or kin.[6] If so, it may be more inclined than the others to sacrifice its life and, along with it, any opportunities for its own reproductive success. Its altruistic genes may cause it to stick its neck out of its hole and warn its relatives that a predator is nearby, but by making this bold gesture it gets caught and consumed by the predator. So its own genes will not get passed on to any offspring. However, by sacrificing itself it gives the altruistic genes that it shares with others in the colony an opportunity to survive and eventually make their way into future generations. So altruistic instincts will get passed on even if the altruistic prairie dog's own genetic future is sacrificed. This genetic understanding of evolution is known as "kin selection." It makes possible inclusive rather than individual fitness.

To those biologists who now accept the notion of inclusive fitness, it is tempting to conclude that no real moral heroism exists anywhere, whether in the lone prairie dog's self-sacrifice or in human expressions of selfless love. This, we admit, is a startling view because theology has always taught that the capacity to lay down one's life for others is the most outstanding human instance of supernatural virtue. Yet among other mammals it now seems that exceptionally heroic acts are purely natural, so why would this not be the case with human

108

mammals as well? Morality, it now appears, can be accounted for in a purely physical rather than spiritual way. Displays of altruism and cooperation are merely the visible expressions of the need that *genes* — which themselves are merely chains of atoms — have for reproductive success. Science has now made it possible to view altruism and cooperative activity as neither virtuous nor sacrificial in any real sense. Virtue is simply a manifestation of blind laws of nature.

But what about our immoral tendencies? Not everybody, after all, is instinctively cooperative. We can be hateful, jealous, and murderous as well. Why so? Our answer is that evolution can account for our immoral impulses too. They are leftovers from the asocial instinctual endowment we have inherited from our remote animal ancestry. Selfish instincts may have been adaptive earlier in evolution, but they are not generally adaptive in social and cultural settings. Nevertheless, they are still rooted in the human genome.

In any case, the moral ideals that have led people to cooperate with one another do not reflect a Platonic heaven. The whole idea of an eternal realm of values is an ingenious, though somewhat circuitous, construct of human genes also. Although you may think of morality as a uniquely human participation in the transcendent goodness of God, your virtuous conduct can be more efficiently explained by science. Cooperation, altruism, and for that matter any inclination to moral behavior are purely natural consequences of a process now brought to the surface by Darwinian biology.

What evolution implies about morality also applies to all the religions of the world. Religions exist not because there is any divine reality, but because nature has selected a pool of human genes that in the prescientific past gave some humans a propensity for religious feelings, thoughts, and actions. The religious instinct was adaptive since it allowed people to believe (falsely) that their lives had an eternal meaning, and this sense of meaning gave them a fictitious motivation to live morally. Apparently humans are still religious today only because religious tendencies proved to be adaptive in our species' genetic past. Because of the biological laws of inheritance we still feel the attraction to belief systems such as those that originally helped adapt our ancestors to harsh environments. Science, however, can now liberate us from the illusion that we need to believe in God in order to be good.

CONTRAST

You will have to go beyond the evolutionary naturalist's shallow explanatory framework to understand why humans are ethical animals. Evolutionary accounts of the development of our moral sense are only weakly illuminating at best. Biology can neither explain nor justify the human ethical attraction to goodness any more than a study of the evolution of mind can account for the universe's intelligibility. Our response to conflict's debunking of theological accounts of morality will show you that morality cannot be fully naturalized after all.

In fact, if you took literally the idea that your own moral inclinations, though modified by cultural factors, are finally reducible to evolutionary adaptation, they would lose all power to motivate you to ethical conduct. An evolutionary interpretation of your own moral aspirations, even if it makes allowance for cultural and historical influences in shaping your conduct, might give you every excuse you need to refuse to cooperate if you don't feel like it. Now that evolutionary naturalists have told you that your moral ideals are ultimately inventions of blind natural selection, why should you continue to be moral?

Any purely evolutionary explanation of morality is self-subverting. There is a logical self-contradiction in conflict's attempt to provide a purely naturalistic explanation of your ethical obligations. To understand our point, start by observing that scientific naturalists themselves follow a profoundly ethical belief system. If you have ever read works by Dawkins, Dennett, Hitchens, Harris, or Flanagan you cannot miss the moral idealism that pervades their popular writings. They consistently and passionately scold their opponents for not adhering to a morally responsible approach to understanding the world. They are especially judgmental toward people of faith for failing to follow the demands of scientism and naturalistic belief. It is *not*

110

right, the New Atheists keep saying, to believe in God.[7] They condemn our belief in God as not only an intellectual but also a moral failing. Their naturalistic ethic, it turns out, is even more puritanical in its moral rigor than that of some religious sects.

However, if the human moral instinct, as evolutionary naturalists maintain, is reducible to adaptation, then how do we know that the New Atheists' own strict morality is anything more than adaptation also? If so, it has no moral authority whatsoever, and we need not pay any attention to it.

Let us explain. Right knowing, according to some prominent scientific naturalists, requires not just cognitive correctness but a purifying process of moral development. We may call this naturalistic set of demands the "ethic of knowledge." The renowned biochemist Jacques Monod (1910–76) is famous for insisting that his readers practice obedience to it. The moral imperative is that all of us *must* submit to the "postulate of objectivity." That is, we are morally obliged to purify our minds of anything other than what is available to scientific method.[8] Similarly, the philosopher W. K. Clifford decreed (in 1877), "It is wrong always, everywhere, and for anyone, to believe anything upon insufficient evidence."[9] Recently the late Christopher Hitchens, resting on his commitment to scientism, repeatedly condemned religion as essentially "immoral."[10] So commitment to scientific naturalism does not dispense with its own code of "rightness" and "wrongness." There can be no doubt that scientific naturalism is profoundly moralistic.

Once again, however, if we accept the evolutionary naturalist's dogma that natural selection and adaptation provide the ultimate explanation of morality, why would this principle not apply also to their own ethic of knowledge? Since naturalism denies the existence of any eternal standard of moral responsibility, why are we obliged to submit to their demand that we should *never* disobey the postulate of objectivity? In other words, how solid is the ground that the naturalists are standing on when they issue their demanding decree that we *must* submit to their ethic of knowledge?

In fact it is logically self-contradictory for naturalists to give you a purely evolutionary account of your own moral aspiration and—in the same breath—declare that their own ethic of knowledge is anything more than an evolutionary adaptation. Why isn't their moral commitment to the ethic of knowledge just as subject to Darwinian debunking as they tell you your own moral ideals are? If so, of course, you need not take them seriously.

Contrast, in response, wants you to obey moral imperatives because they are inherently good, not because they are adaptive. The idea of evolutionary adaptation cannot justify moral obedience to anything. After all, deception and sexual promiscuity can be adaptive in a genetic sense. So also celibacy and martyrdom can contribute to inclusive fitness. By explaining a whole spectrum of mutually contradictory behavioral instincts in terms of adaptation, evolutionary accounts of morality end up explaining or justifying none of them.

So, if evolutionary science cannot explain or justify your moral commitments, then what can? To be sure, natural, social, and personal history is involved in the shaping of your conscience. But, something in addition to evolutionary and cultural influences must be involved in the awakening of a truly serious sense of responsibility. Just as something more than evolutionary science is needed to justify your trust that the universe is intelligible (see chapter 7), so also something other than Darwinian theory is needed to justify your commitment to goodness. Contrast, therefore, proposes that an *adequate* grounding of your moral life can come only from a view of reality that includes a theological dimension at its foundation. It is because the deepest core of your personal existence has already been touched by an infinite and eternal goodness that in the course of your lifetime you gradually awaken to moral responsibility.

This awakening of your moral sense, however, takes place in stages. One of our biggest objections to simplistic Darwinian accounts of morality is that they overlook the fact that the moral sense develops only gradually. Morality can refer to a wide range of behavioral traits and dispositions as people grow from childhood into adulthood. The process of moral maturation involves prolonged periods of struggle and countless setbacks in the transition from selfishness to selflessness. So if evolutionary naturalists expect biological explanations of human morality to be illuminating, they would have to take each distinct stage of moral development into account.

However, they fail to do so. All the different levels of moral motivation are given the same ultimate explanation: adaptation. Some Darwinians allow that cultural influences can reverse our crudest natural behavioral instincts. But the "ultimate" explanation of morality, they still insist, can be found only in evolutionary biology.[11] Once again, by trying to explain all stages of human moral commitment in terms of adaptation, evolutionary accounts of morality explain none.

For the sake of simplicity we may delineate three levels of moral development: preconventional, conventional, and postconventional stages.[12]

The Preconventional Stage of Moral Development

In its most elementary or "preconventional" stage, human conduct is shaped by a sense of rewards and punishments. Children learn to behave themselves if they realize there are rewards and punishments associated with different kinds of action. Maybe evolutionary biology has something to contribute to our understanding of this earliest stage in the moral growth process. The need for gratification and the aversion to pain are surely adaptive traits without which human genes would never have much chance to survive. So just for the sake of argument let us concede that childish morality may be understood, at least partly, in terms of evolutionary adaptation.

The Conventional Stage of Moral Development

A second phase of moral development—let us call it "conventional" morality—is based on a natural longing to become accepted by a social group of one kind or another. This group may be one's family, gang, classmates, sorority, workmates, church community, military unit, political party, and so on. No doubt we have a natural need to belong, as do many other species of life. There is poignant evidence of belongingness, for example, in recent studies of primates.[13] The need to belong requires cooperation, and so this second level of moral development may also allow, in part, for a biological interpretation.

113

The Postconventional Stage of Moral Development

Even if the first two stages of moral development could be explained in evolutionary terms, however, at least some people reach a stage of moral (and religious) development that completely befuddles the naturalist's dream of providing ultimate evolutionary explanation. We may call this stage "postconventional" morality (and religion).[14] At this level human conduct is based on a sense of universal, unconditional values. Postconventional morality is rooted in the conviction that certain actions are intrinsically and unconditionally good, regardless of the consequences to oneself or one's group stability. Obedience to such values may even lead to uncooperative and maladaptive behavior, at times destabilizing a group and causing social turmoil. Conduct motivated by a sense of unconditional values—say, truth, love, justice, or peace—may even be considered evil from the perspective of a purely conventional morality.

In the Abrahamic traditions, for example, the "prophet" is a figure who disturbs the status quo and professes belief in a God of the poor and marginalized. The God of the prophets—the God of Israel, Christianity, and Islam—stands up for the rights of society's outcasts. People who follow the prophetic ideal of morality often end up being persecuted and sometimes even executed by those ensconced comfortably within the narrowness of a conventional setting. The prophet, a figure that all three Abrahamic faiths enshrine as the ideal, is a person who testifies to having been grasped by what is imperishably and absolutely good. The prophet insists that universal or eternal values have placed unconditional demands on all of us.

It goes without saying, of course, that sustaining a postconventional moral posture is not easy. The pressures to conform are enormous. The prophets in our midst lead maladaptive moral lives, often refusing to cooperate with those whose moral lives remain stuck at either of the first two levels. Darwinian moralists will attempt to explain even exceptionally heroic morality in terms of adaptation and kin selection. But, as we noted earlier, explanations that account for every instance of morality in terms of the same causal factors fail to account for any. An evolutionary naturalist, for example, who explains

114

both conformist Nazi morality and postconventional anti-Nazi resist-ance in exactly the same causal terms (adaptation or kin selection) has not said anything helpful about morality at all.

Even if preconventional or conventional behavior contributes to gene survival (which is not impossible), citing this fact does not explain what is unique about the prophetic type. Gene transmission is too general an idea to account for all the different levels of motivation that shape human morality. The laws of thermodynamics, to use an analogy, are operative whether the temperature is hot or cold outside today, and so perhaps in one sense it is not wrong to say that heat exchanges are the explanation of the weather in both instances. This kind of explanation is not wrong, but it is empty. Similarly, genetic transmission is going on whether people are being bad or good, cow-ardly or heroic. But something other than gene survival will have to be called upon to account for the differences.[15]

CONVERGENCE

Even though natural selection alone cannot account for our attraction to goodness, we may still fruitfully adopt an evolutionary perspective on human morality. The evolution of morality, like that of the awakening of intelligence, is a momentous new chapter in the drama of the universe. Our cosmic perspective on the meaning of intelligence and faith carries over to our understanding of moral aspi-ration as well.

The moral instinct is not necessarily the consequence of a divine command planted immediately in each person's mind independently of our natural and social existence. Nor is our moral sensitivity based on a faint *remembrance* of a Platonic realm of perfection from which the soul has been temporarily exiled. These classic theological pro-posals are understandable in a pre-Darwinian age. Moreover, they each point to the inadequacy of a purely naturalistic justification of morality. They express the correct intuition that moral obedience means allowing ourselves to *be grasped* by an eternal goodness. Nevertheless, in view of what we now know about the evolution of life and mind, we need to place morality also in the setting of a universe that is still coming into being.

With Plato, Aquinas, and Kant, convergence agrees that our existence is oriented toward a transcendent *goodness*. But our orientation toward an eternal goodness is one of the ways by which we participate in the long journey of the whole universe into God. We need not think of God as standing above the world, continually measuring the inevitable insufficiency of human attempts "down here" to imitate an eternal perfection "up there." Our moral existence would be most disheartening if that were all there is to it. All the ages of human moral striving would add up to very little if human virtue were only a matter of imitating a timeless perfection. It would be mostly a record of failure. The perfectionist approach to moral life has sometimes led to a paralyzing sense of guilt and even self-rejection: We never measure up, and so we hate ourselves. Perfectionism has understandably provoked the reaction known as "atheism."

No doubt our moral life requires our following exemplars of goodness, but our aspiration to live a good life is most alive when we have a sense that our existence and actions can make a real difference in the world. An evolutionary perspective on morality, we suggest, can give a cosmic significance to our moral actions that was inconceivable in the framework of a static universe.

For this reason, convergence invites you in this age of science to think of your moral life as one of anticipation, not just imitation. We mean simply that you can become excited about your moral life if you first have a realistic hope that your life and actions can truly matter to the world that is still emerging and of which you are a part. You will be more inclined to be good if you first have a sense that you are contributing something significant to the ongoing work of creation. Even the simplest and most monotonous of your labors can become more bearable if you understand them as playing a part in a larger and lasting enterprise. Only a "zest for living" can sustain your moral efforts for long. But a zest for living thrives on the anticipation that something of great importance is going on in the cosmic drama into which you have been born.[16]

Instead of abandoning you to the feeling of being condemned by the moral perfectionists, therefore, our narrative-evolutionary understanding of the universe continually opens up a new future of ethical opportunity. Moral conversion, once you come to realize that the universe is still being created, does not mean wallowing in self-accusation and regret. Rather it means diving back into the stream of creativity into which you have come to life in the first place.[17] If the universe were not going anywhere, if it were just standing still, then your moral life would be reduced to imitation of exemplars of virtue and striving for personal perfection. But the cosmos, as we have been emphasizing, is still coming into being, and you are part of this becoming. Science has unwittingly made a great contribution to the grounding of human morality by uncovering the great story of cosmic creativity into which you may now pour your own moral choices and commitments.

We are not denying the ethical importance of imitation and pursuit of virtue. But suppose you become aware that your life, your work, and your way of relating to others can make a difference, however small, in a drama of cosmic proportions. Then your imitation of moral heroes and your quest to be virtuous take on the enlivening new dimension of hopeful anticipation that something of consequence is taking shape up ahead in the cosmic future. Your moral life, then, need not be one of just spinning your wheels while waiting to be swept up into heaven. Morality is not exclusively a matter of self-improvement or preparing your soul for entrance into another world. It is a matter of participation in creation.

If you can learn to locate your moral action in the context of a still unfinished universe, you will understand the importance of virtue to the building of what Jews and Christians have called the "kingdom of God." You will see your life not just as imitation but also as cooperation with God in the work of creation. Faith's role, as it was for the prophets of old, is to open up a new future on which you can spend your efforts. Without such hope in the future the prophetic ideal of moral existence will decay into conventional moralism, unrealistic perfectionism, and cosmic escapism.[18]

Neither conflict nor contrast can provide an appropriate framework for robust ethical existence. By declaring that the universe and all human effort lead to nothing in the end, conflict can only weaken your motivation and diminish the scope of your moral endeavors. If the universe is ultimately pointless, the best you can salvage from it morally is an individualistic tragic heroism that requires a Promethean courage to resist the inevitable. Perhaps there is something honorable in facing the apparent absurdity of the universe. More often than not, however, conflict's sense of cosmic futility offers little to prevent the flight from responsibility altogether.

Contrast, for its part, still finds moral motivation enough in an otherworldly theological vision that has both challenged and attracted countless believers over many centuries. Following ancient ideas of the philosopher Plato and the dualism still resident in modern culture, the contrast approach assumes that there is a transcendent world of perfect goodness (God) beyond our present world of becoming and perishing. Moral life in such a setting strives to imitate the saints who have detached themselves from the world in order to be closer to God. Needless to say, contrast has little interest in connecting our ethical lives to the ongoing work of cosmic becoming and creativity. Even though today contrast accepts evolution and astrophysics as valid sciences, its followers are not concerned to link either faith or morality to the cosmic journey itself.

For convergence, however, moral aspiration is part of the same dramatic cosmic awakening that has given rise to intelligence and freedom. The sense of being called to responsibility is inseparable from the anticipatory cosmic drama that bears you along. It is the world's own thrust toward deeper complexity and *more being* up ahead that can truly energize moral animals. Because our moral lives are part of a massive cosmic movement of *becoming more*, we cannot escape the forward thrust of the drama that gave birth to us. We humans experience this anticipatory cosmic restlessness consciously in the form of intelligence, moral aspiration, and the quest for beauty.

The insatiable search for intelligibility and truth, the aesthetic attraction to more intense beauty, and the moral quest for goodness are all clearly anticipatory. Intelligence feeds on an emerging coherence that it anticipates but has not yet reached. Aesthetic awareness is kindled by a vague intuition that a more intense beauty awaits us beyond our present grasp. And moral awareness arises ultimately because of our reaching out toward a goodness that grasps us more than we can grasp it. Convergence suggests, however, that these anticipatory experiences make the most sense when we situate them within an unfinished universe.

This cosmos that gave birth to us has always been open to *becoming more*. Through the human mind the universe anticipates an inexhaustible meaning and truth. Through our aesthetic restlessness the universe is now opening itself to an endless beauty. And through our moral sensitivity it is awakening to an infinite goodness. What faith adds to this cosmic stirring is a trust that meaning, truth, beauty, and goodness are *everlasting*. And if they are everlasting, then we can be assured that our responses to them not only matter, but that they matter forever.

CHAPTER 9

Are We Special?

CONFLICT

No! We are the product of blind chance and impersonal physical necessity. The laws of physics and chemistry, along with the biological mechanism of natural selection, are sufficient to explain our existence. There
is no evidence that the universe cares for us or that an intelligent deity
intended our being here. The odds against our existence are enormous,
so it's no wonder we feel a bit strange here. You may believe that since
you have a mind, and your mind seems so different from mindless matter, you are exempt from the overall cosmic indifference. But your existence is completely unremarkable as far as science is concerned. Your
mental and moral activity can be explained in purely material terms, as
we have already clarified. Given enough time—and there has been
time aplenty—a combination of accidents and blind physical laws can
bring living, thinking, and moral beings into existence for a brief season
in the immensity of cosmic history. But eventually the era of consciousness—including your own precarious mental life—will be blotted out
for good in the cold collapse of the material universe. Then it will be as
though persons had never existed. How then could anyone seriously
claim that we are special?

Matter could just as easily have existed indefinitely in numerous
configurations without any trace of mind, the quality that makes us
seem special. The Big Bang universe got along quite well without
thinking beings for nearly 14 billion mindless years before we showed
up. Physical reality cares not a whit whether mind pops up in the cosmos at all. The presence of intelligent beings in the universe is the
 result of a very unlikely departure from matter's essential state of

mindlessness. From conflict's materialist point of view, human minds sometimes seem like alien intruders.

Imagining, then, that your own existence is any more privileged than that of rocks and radishes shows how far out of touch you are with science. However, you need not feel sad about science's displacement of the Earth and human beings from the illusion of centrality. If it seems at first that science is bad news, you're taking it the wrong way. In fact, the dethronement of religiously sponsored anthropocentrism is one of the great benefits of modern science. To learn now that you are not special can deliver you from the burden of submission to a fictitious lawgiving deity and from the needless guilt that accompanies a false sense of self-importance. Conflict takes for granted that everything that happens in the universe, including the appearance of your mind, is the consequence of impersonal physical laws. Your existence as an intelligent being is not the product of some eternal design. No personal deity planned for you to be here or supervises your life now.

Consequently, we are especially disturbed these days by the recent misuse of astrophysics, even by some scientists, to restore humanity to a more privileged perch in the universe than even religions had assumed. To be specific, we consider it our duty to warn you about the seductive new allure of some interpretations of what is called the "Anthropic Principle" (AP). AP makes the allegedly scientific claim that the eventual emergence of "mind," or the arrival in cosmic history of intelligent beings like us, was already in the cards during the earliest moments of the cosmic story. The term Anthropic is derived from *anthropos*, the Greek word for human being. So AP may seem to suggest that the entire cosmic story was carefully set up from the start to give birth eventually to us, or at least to intelligent beings like us. The universe, as physicist Freeman Dyson wishfully reflects, seems to have known from the start "that we were coming."[1]

AP assumes that the Big Bang universe's initial physical conditions and fundamental constants had to be "just right" or "fine-tuned" from the start if life and mind were to come into our universe nearly 14 billion years later. So to some scientists AP in effect claims that our own existence is special after all.[2] In our opinion, nothing could be more unscientific or self-serving than the idea that this whole vast universe was made to give rise to human beings, as some interpretations of AP seem to suggest. Of course, we agree that the existence of our minds is unintelligible apart from specific initial cosmic conditions and constants. Even materialist scientists can accept a Weak Anthropic Principle (WAP), which simply observes that the existence of life and mind is compatible with only a definite set of physical factors and mathematical values.

What we reject is the claim that these properties were fine-tuned, presumably by God, for the purpose of producing special beings endowed with minds. In other words, we reject the Theological Anthropic Principle (TAP). If TAP is correct, and the universe was intentionally fine-tuned for life and mind, we confess that it would challenge our naturalistic worldview and justify the belief that we are special after all. In our opinion, however, TAP is wishful thinking rather than respectable science. In the interest of fairness, however, let us examine AP more closely and let you draw your own conclusions about whether it has any theological implications.

AP stems from the belief that fundamental features of the universe, such as the force of gravity and the rate of cosmic expansion, have a much closer relationship to the existence of life and mind than modern science had ever known prior to the last half of the twentieth century. If life and mind were ever to arise in our universe, for example, a delicate balancing act between the force of gravity and the rate of cosmic expansion must have been present from the very first microseconds of the Big Bang universe's existence. The existence of carbon, with its special bonding properties, is essential to the production of organic molecules, the building blocks of life, and living cells and human brains could not exist without carbon. However—and here is where you have to avoid being brainwashed by theology—if the universe had expanded only slightly faster or slower than it has, the kind of massive stars that cooked up carbon and other elements essential to life and mind could never have formed. Could this exquisitely precise initial calibration of cosmic numbers, this "fine-tuning" of the physics of the early universe, be just a mindless accident?

122

Proponents of TAP think not, and in doing so they claim that
they have made room for divine design: a creator God set up the universe from the start so that it would allow for our existence. People of
faith, as you can see, resort to the wildest ideas to support their longing for significance. Conflict, however, thinks the cause of the fine-
tuning was sheer accident.

Other features of the nascent universe, according to AP, also had
to be "just right" if mind were ever to show up in our universe. For
example, the ratio of electron to proton mass, the amplitude of the rip-
ples in early cosmic radiation, and the ratio of the weak to the strong
nuclear force had to be exactly what they are if our universe was ever
going to give rise to life and intelligence.[3] Conflict can accept all of this.

The interesting question, however, is *why* the physical values are just
right for cells and brains. Because of God, or because of chance and blind
physical necessity? Contrary to our skeptical position, TAP claims that the
universe was fine-tuned from the start by a good and intelligent deity. The
physical values were set with such precision that carbon-based life and
persons with minds could eventually and inevitably come onto the cosmic scene. Billions of years before mind appeared, divine intelligence
determined precisely the mathematical values of the physical conditions
and constants that would give rise to us. So we are special after all.

Conflict, however, offers you a simpler explanation than TAP:
the cosmic "fine-tuning" is due to chance alone. Our purely natural
way of explaining the physics of the early universe allows for no invok-
ing of deities, miracles, or gratuitous leaps of faith. Let us call our
explanation the "Random Anthropic Principle" (RAP). By RAP we
mean that the assembling of the set of precise numbers that allows our
universe to give birth to mind is purely accidental. Yes, the numerical
values have to be "just right," but they are just right because of chance
rather than divine design.

So, you ask, How could such an improbable arrangement of
physical properties—all of which might have been different individu-
ally—have come together by chance rather than design in our universe's earliest moments? Our answer, because science cannot use
God as an explanation of anything, is the idea of a "multiverse." We

hypothesize the existence of countless universes, most of which would not have the physical coincidences that allow for life and mind. Our purely naturalistic proposal is that if there are enough universes, eventually a mind-bearing one will pop up in this lavish lottery. The multiverse postulates an unimaginably large number of separate worlds as the widest setting in which the improbable existence of a mind-bearing universe could, in all this statistical immensity, become possible and even probable without any divine intervention.

From the conflict perspective, therefore, TAP is an outpouring of nonsense devised to shore up, with the apparent help of physics and cosmology, our childish sense of self-importance. Although some scientists find TAP intriguing, we consider it outrageously unscientific compared to the bolder and more intellectually adventurous RAP. TAP also runs against the grain of scientific method by trying to explain a chronologically earlier set of occurrences (the initial cosmological conditions and fundamental constants) in terms of results (life and mind) that don't appear until much later in time—indeed billions of years later! How then can you call TAP "explanation" in any genuine sense of the term? Good science holds that only those events that chronologically precede and lead up to subsequent events may be called explanatory. TAP is simply a desperate attempt to justify human vanity. It merits no further consideration by self-respecting scientists.

CONTRAST

We are not enthusiastic about either TAP or RAP. We believe that humans are special, but we don't need science to support this belief. Science, by the very nature of its value-neutral method of inquiry, is incapable of making anything look special. In fact, the whole objective of science is to show that what at first seems remarkable is, upon analysis, quite unremarkable. Faith alone, not scientific cosmology, is what justifies our sense of God's special love and care for us. How big or how old the universe is—or even how many worlds there are—remains completely irrelevant to our sense of personal value. Faith teaches us that each person is unique and special in God's sight. Our encounter in faith with the personal God of prophetic religions is ultimately what gives us a sense of our eternal value and dignity. Science has nothing to tell us one way or another about our self-worth.

Contrast therefore wants nothing to do with either TAP or RAP. It is not for scientific but theological reasons that we ignore both versions of AP. Attempts to validate God's existence or establish the true identity of human beings scientifically is theologically repugnant, especially because science can deal only with objects rather than subjects, and because science changes so much from one age to the next. Any "God" that science appears to have discovered can be nothing more than an empty abstraction. Such a deity would not be the living God of Abrahamic faith. It would be a "god of the gaps," not the challenging and redemptive personal God of Moses, Jesus, or Muhammad. We reject RAP because it arbitrarily excludes any role for divine providence, and we ignore TAP because it is no more able to transform our lives and deepen our faith than are the cold classical design arguments for God's existence. If you want to know what the universe is really all about you are more likely to find it on display in a single act of human kindness than by searching all the stars or studying all the theories and equations of astrophysics.[4]

Furthermore, appreciating our specialness requires a realization that, contrary to both TAP and RAP, we humans do *not* fit comfortably into the cosmos. Our faith tells us that human persons should not look for reasons to become adjusted to the material world. We are "strangers and foreigners on the earth" as the Christian author of the Letter to the Hebrews puts it (11:13). Even cognitive scientists know how hard it is to find an intelligible place for mind and personality in a mindless material universe. Thought and physical reality differ so completely from each other that any attempt to unify them is destined to misunderstand both. Modern materialists have tried but failed miserably to eliminate the irreducible immateriality of our minds and souls. And theologians who seek too tight a synthesis of mind and matter are likely to compromise their allegiance to reality's spiritual dimension. In other words, any purely scientific study of minds and persons easily leads back to the dead end of materialism.

Materialist accounts of mind are not only intellectually but also morally repugnant. By attempting to reduce our minds to purely physical stuff, contemporary materialists such as Daniel Dennett in effect turn persons into valueless objects. Materialists are typically unaware of the fact that their worldview has given intellectual legitimacy to the unprecedented depersonalization and even massacre of millions upon millions of human beings by twentieth-century despots and their followers. Materialist reductionism has allowed modern thought to lose any sense of the intimate connection each self has with the eternal. Materialism thus destroys the only reliable basis for upholding a sense of human dignity. Once our link to an infinite goodness became lost to modern secularist thought we no longer had any moral defense against the slaughter of countless human beings by dictators and social engineers to whom personal dignity was no more than a pious illusion.

It is unfortunate, therefore, that today many scientific thinkers still look for ways to make human existence seem even more unexceptional than ever. One example of this leveling obsession is the reductionist habit of looking upon human life as physical "simplicity masquerading as complexity." But another is the misleading appeal to the "Copernican Principle," which since the seventeenth century has increasingly emphasized how "average" and cosmically insignificant the Earth is in the solar system and the wider universe. Copernicus decentralized our planet from its apparently special place in the scheme of things. Accordingly, the Copernican Principle highlights the fact that science has brought about a whole series of decentralizations that challenge human specialness.

To start with, our planet is no longer the center around which the sun and other planets rotate. It is merely an "average" planet in terms of size and location. So, according to the Copernican Principle, neither the Earth nor its inhabitants can be called special. Then, in the twentieth century astronomers have shown that the sun and planets are no more than a mediocre physical system in an average arm of an average spiral galaxy (the Milky Way) that comprises billions of stars and (probably) even more planets. Most recently the Copernican Principle took over even more territory when the Hubble telescope disclosed that the observable universe contains as many as 200 billion galaxies. Our galaxy too, therefore, now seems only average.

So what is the next stage in the Copernican Principle's progress? You have just seen it earlier in this chapter. It is conflict's appeal to the idea of a multiverse. So addicted is conflict to the idea of our own insignificance that, without the slightest shred of evidence, it has swallowed whole the latest trendy speculation that there must be an indefinitely large number of "universes" beyond the observable one we live in. So, not just humanity, but also our whole Big Bang universe is now unremarkable. Our mind-bearing universe is just what we should expect if there are enough mindless universes hidden behind it statistically.

What is the contrast response to this relentless march of mediocrity? Has science now demonstrated that we humans are even more "average" than we had even remotely suspected? Not at all! As far as contrast is concerned, the whole exuberant scientific display of cosmic immensity and multiplicity does nothing to diminish the specialness of conscious, free, moral human subjects. In fact, our personal uniqueness stands out all the more sharply when contrasted with the ever-widening scientific display of mindlessness. Why would anyone suppose that our diminutive physical size or our "average" location in the total scheme of things is a reason for denying our irreplaceable personal value? It matters not an iota where or when consciousness and freedom entered into God's creation. Mind, spirit, freedom, and personhood are so distinct from the general condition of cosmic impersonality that people of faith need not look for any great theological significance in the new astrophysical expansion of our physical horizons, imaginary or not.

Nevertheless, we want to make it clear that contrast has no reason to deny the existence of a multiverse. For all we know, the existence of innumerable universes is completely consistent with string theory or other novel ideas in physics. The idea of a multiverse is also in keeping with the extravagantly overflowing generosity of the creator

God in whom we already believe. But this is beside the point. What interests us here, and what calls for explanation, is the *motivation* behind the fashionable current push by scientific naturalists to widen the ambiance of the Copernican Principle. Why, even in the absence of empirical evidence, has there been such a noticeable surge lately in astrophysical speculation about the existence of numberless worlds?[5] Even though so far there is no physical evidence of a multiverse, this has not stopped allegedly scientific thinkers from making the multiverse central to their philosophies of nature. Why so?

We suggest that the new multiverse rage, at least among those who embrace conflict, has less to do with science than with an attraction to a materialist worldview in which our own existence is ultimately insignificant. The easiest way to give this depersonalizing belief scientific stature is to interpret the Copernican Principle as proof that human existence is unremarkable on any scale. And one way to do that is to show that our universe, with all its anthropic fine-tuning, is itself unremarkable when all is said and done. An unending plurality or succession of worlds would apparently allow for the probability that at least one fine-tuned, mind-bearing universe might emerge—accidentally and unsurprisingly—from the whole batch. In that case there would be nothing special about the arrival of mind on Earth because there is nothing surprising, first of all, about the existence of a mind-bearing universe. Contrast finds this kind of reasoning to be itself most remarkable. It is an extraordinarily awkward way of carrying out the materialist project of denying the incalculable value of personal existence.

Finally, proponents of conflict almost invariably make the mistake of assuming that pre-Copernican geocentrism—where the Earth is the center around which everything else revolves—was an expression of religious presumption and human arrogance. In effect, however, placing the Earth in the center of universe made it the world's garbage dump, a collector of cosmic debris rather than an especially privileged place. The sublunary location of our planet made it the lowliest rather than the most important region in the universe. The higher levels of being, including the sun and stars, exist beyond the moon. So when Copernicus and

Galileo put the sun in the center where the Earth had been and placed the Earth in orbit around the sun, this readjustment amounted to a demotion of the heavens, not a deflation of human vanity.

CONVERGENCE

AP is controversial, whether in the form of TAP or RAP, but in all of its versions it brings out how intimately the human mind is woven into the long cosmic story. Whether by divine design or sheer chance, it is clearer now than ever that beings endowed with minds are the outcome of a long narrative process. Unlike contrast, however, convergence finds it theologically exciting, and not at all distressful, that our minds are inseparable from the cosmos. The existence of thought, we now realize, is tied tightly to the configuration of physical properties in the Big Bang universe. Whether a creator God has a role in this setup or not, it is now undeniable that the building of brains and minds began about 14 billion years ago. Does the new scientific sense of the inseparability of your mind from the material universe dissolve your sense of self-worth? Or does it not instead elevate the whole cosmic story, and you along with it, to a level of value and importance that has escaped the notice of both conflict and contrast?

Conflict tries to suppress your sense of specialness by reducing you to mindless stuff. Contrast, in order to protect you from such diminishment, tries (unsuccessfully) to locate your mind in a special place apart from the material universe. Convergence, however, firmly rejects—on both theological and scientific grounds—any loosening of the ties between your mind and the physical universe. We suggest that by being linked to a still unfinished cosmic story, human specialness consists at least partly of our contributing to the great drama of a universe just now awakening into thought, freedom, and moral aspiration. Our special vocation, at least from a dramatic cosmological perspective, is that each of us is called upon to foster and participate in this awakening.

To convergence the universe hangs together in an intelligible way—not in the manner of a mechanism, which our limited human minds might prefer, but in the manner of a story that is not yet finished. Consequently, grasping the meaning or intelligibility of the cosmic story requires a different mind-set from that of trying to understand the design of a machine, cell, or organism. It requires *waiting* in patient expectation for the meaning of the story to reveal itself. Narrative coherence, unlike mechanical design, also demands that we allow ourselves to be swept up into the story or carried away by it if we want to understand it. A purely objective, detached, and impersonal disposition will only conceal the story's meaning from us.

Since the cosmic narrative is still being written, therefore, any meaning it might have can be fully revealed only in the future, perhaps the far distant future. The universe's intelligibility lies mostly beyond the range of our vision here and now. Science cannot decipher this meaning. Scientific analysis by itself leads our minds downward into the cellular, molecular, or atomic makeup of things, and this analysis simultaneously carries us back in time toward the cosmic past—before life and mind existed. But what the cosmic story is finally all about, as we shall propose again in chapter 11, is not a question that science can answer. Nor is it a question that faith and theology can answer either. What faith and theology can do is keep our minds and hearts trained on the future and open to surprise. Whatever narrative coherence the cosmic story might have can be approached at present only in a spirit of hope and expectation.

Convergence, therefore, asks not about the mechanical design of particular objects and organisms but about the meaning of the drama of life and the universe. Because we are concerned with dramatic meaning rather than the physical anatomy of nature, we have no difficulty theologically accepting the "design flaws" in evolutionary adaptations. After all, if every present design in the life-world were perfect, life would be fixed and frozen. There would be no story, no drama, and no openness to a new future. Everything would be dead.

Convergence believes that prophetic, Abrahamic faith can awaken us to the *promise* of meaning. Only the posture of expectation or anticipation can turn our minds toward the kind of intelligibility the cosmic story may be carrying. It is only in the future that the cosmos, which has sometimes been called "the greatest story ever told," can yield its full meaning and identity. Faith's function is to keep us looking in hope toward that future, even if any grasp of it seems far off. If the universe were supposed to be fully intelligible here and now we might have reason to complain that things are not perfect. But if the universe is still coming into being, and if the story is still unfolding, we must be patient. Teaching patience has always been a central concern of our faith traditions.

The universe, therefore, is not structured in the manner proposed by TAP, which assumes that God is an engineer or divine designer. Nor is randomness the sole factor in the initial cosmic configuration, as RAP supposes. Rather, our universe is an exquisite blend of accident, predictable "grammatical" rules, and time, the three essential elements of any story. What this means is that the universe follows what we may call the "Narrative Anthropic Principle" (NAP).[6] The universe was made to give rise to stories. NAP pulls together something from both TAP and RAP, but its focus is on the dramatic character of the universe. NAP accepts TAP's assumption that the universe is intelligible and that mind is an essential aspect of the universe rather than a purely accidental blip in the cosmic story. But it also accepts RAP's intuition that everything in the cosmos emerges from the interplay of randomness, reliability, and time.[7] These three ingredients are the stuff of story, and they are foundational to our understanding of the Big Bang universe—and even a multiverse if it exists.

The narrative blend of accident, law, and time, as we saw in chapter 3, provides the cosmic setting in which Darwinian evolution takes place. Evolution, therefore, is simply an expression at the level of life of the more fundamental Narrative Anthropic Principle that gives the universe its essentially dramatic character. Convergence does not look for God *primarily* in an initial cosmic design or in organic and subcellular complexity. Our search for God requires a search for the meaning of the whole cosmic story. However, we cannot expect to make complete sense of the universe here and now, especially if we are narrowly focused on the intricacies of nature's designs. Meaning is carried not by design but by stories.

SCIENCE AND FAITH

Because the cosmic drama is still unfinished, science is not yet in a position to grasp its narrative coherence in a complete and final way. The quest for cosmic meaning requires putting on the habit of hope. It is part of our own specialness that in human beings the cosmic story has finally become conscious of itself, and it can now deliberately open itself in anticipation of what may be taking shape up ahead. Science and faith are distinct ways of reading the story. Science tells us about the narrative's alphabet, lexicon, and grammar. Faith and theology look for the story's meaning. We don't expect to find meaning in architectural perfection, and we are not interested only in a reverse engineering that digs back into the makeup of natural phenomena. It is the proper role of analytical science to do this. Convergence, for its part, can grasp meaning only by anticipation, not by direct sight. We must wait for it in prayerful patience. This is both our duty and our dignity.

CHAPTER 10

Is There Life after Death?

CONFLICT

Scientific naturalism—the worldview that conflict follows throughout this book—predicts that your consciousness will not survive your death. Those of us who take the conflict approach generally embrace the materialist (or physicalist) claim that nothing other than matter exists. Ideas such as soul, spirit, and God are at best adaptive fictions. When you die your consciousness will vanish into a mindless void from which it will never awaken. Many billions, or perhaps even trillions, of years from now the Big Bang universe itself will also fade into the same eternal sleep. Every instance of sentience and consciousness in the cosmos will expire utterly. Nothing and nobody will remain to remember any trace of it. Your destiny, like that of the whole universe, is nothingness.

Duke University naturalist philosopher Owen Flanagan accurately represents our conflict perspective on the question of an afterlife. He admits that the majority of people on our planet still believe in life after death. He points out quite rightly, however, that this belief is irrational because science can provide no evidence to support it. After all, science is the only trustworthy way to get to the truth about things, and it has found not a shred of evidence that an afterlife awaits us. Not only is belief in immortality irrational, says Flanagan, it is also an impediment to the spread of naturalism: "Most philosophers and scientists in the twenty-first century see their job as making the world safe for a fully naturalistic view of things. The beliefs in nonnatural properties of persons, indeed of any nonnatural things, including—yes—God, stand in the way of understanding our natures truthfully...."[1]

Flanagan, a respected contemporary philosopher, argues convincingly that the "humanistic image" of ourselves as spiritual beings endowed with free will and an immortal soul is intellectually obsolete. We are neither free nor do we have souls. Flanagan endorses the more realistic "scientific image" that entails a materialist worldview. The scientific image should now replace the humanistic image. "One image says humans are possessed of a spiritual part—an incorporeal mind or soul—and that one's life and eternal fate turn on the fate of this soul. The other image says that there is no such thing as the soul and thus that nothing—nothing at all—depends on its state." The rational person is obliged to accept the conclusions of scientific naturalism: "When we die, we—or better, the particles that once composed us—return to nature's bosom, not to God's right hand."[2]

Why then, you may be asking, is belief in life after death still so persistent, even in a scientific age? How can so many people be so completely wrong? Darwin, once again, can help us answer this question. Belief in immortality is deeply embedded in our nature ultimately because it has been adaptive in an evolutionary sense. Hope for immortality led our religious ancestors in the remote past to embrace the fiction that we each have an *eternal* worth and destiny. This false conviction gave them a reason to live ethical lives. They expected to be rewarded by God after death for good deeds and feared they would be punished for bad. Belief in immortality allowed our ancestors to cling to the illusion that their lives matter eternally. The religious expectation of immortal existence made them want to cooperate with others during their lifetimes. Seen from an evolutionary point of view, cooperation with other members of your species makes it more likely that you—or at least your kin—will live long enough to mate, bear offspring, and thus pass on cooperative genes to future generations. Belief in immortality, even though it is irrational, has been good for gene survival. This is why it persists.

People today have inherited the cooperative genes that programmed our ancestors to live moral lives. These genes continue to build brains that have a weakness for believing in an afterlife. Consequently, even today the illusion of immortality, like the sense of

God, won't go quietly away. Evolutionary biology more than any other set of scientific ideas explains why humans still imagine they have imperishable souls that can survive into a deathless beyond. So scientific skeptics like us will have a hard time convincing people of faith that their hopes are in vain.

This is why some of us who embrace the conflict position are less scornful of human religious tendencies than are Dawkins and the other New Atheists. We now realize that the inclination to believe in an afterlife is built into our genetic makeup and that it has been adaptive for previous human generations. Even though belief in life beyond death is unacceptable to scientifically educated people today, we are sympathetic enough to recognize that without religion's adaptive qualities our ancestors would never have survived and we would not be here today. Even though we are convinced that the idea of immortality is entirely fictitious, we are not terribly disturbed that this illusion continues to flourish.[3] As long as it promotes the survival of human genes it has a biological value even if it is contrary to scientific reason.

CONTRAST

It is not surprising that adherents of scientism deny any prospect of conscious life after death. But who says scientism is right? We have shown in previous chapters that scientism itself is an unscientific belief. Scientism is self-contradictory and hence irrational. Scientism tells you to take nothing on faith, and yet it takes faith to embrace scientism. So who is being unreasonable here? Is it those of us who believe in life after death, or those who embrace the self-contradictory doctrine of scientism?

Anyway, Flanagan and others who reject belief in an afterlife have seldom looked carefully at what their materialist worldview really implies. The great American psychologist and philosopher William James, however, expressed in unforgettable language what materialism really means. It means that once something perishes it is "gone utterly from the very sphere and room of being. Without an echo; without a memory; without an influence on aught that may come after, to make it care for similar ideals. This utter final wreck and tragedy is of the essence of scientific materialism as at present understood."[4]

Scientific materialists such as Flanagan are logically required to agree with this sober assessment: Life and mind are *ultimately* of no value or significance because eventually nothing will remain of them. Most people throughout the ages, however, have deeply valued their existence. For them the final extinguishing of mind and spirit would be the greatest of evils. The possibility that consciousness or personality could end up in the pit of absolute nothingness, as scientific materialism implies, is both unthinkable and morally deadening. Our own belief that people have immortal souls allows us to reverence each person as eternally valuable. When modern thought made the idea of an immortal soul questionable it allowed the likes of Stalin, Hitler, and Mao to exterminate vast numbers of their fellow human beings as intrinsically worthless. Furthermore, the idea that everyone has an immortal soul allows us to value the weak, the handicapped, the sick, the elderly, and the mentally disturbed. All persons are everlastingly precious in the eyes of God and therefore deserving of our reverence. If you eliminate the idea of the soul you open the door to the most monstrous forms of evil.

No doubt, belief in immortality has not always prevented religious believers from slaughtering one another—often in the name of God. Religious people are often guilty of enormous hatred, repression, violence, and murder. Yet in terms of sheer body count it is doubtful that in all the centuries of religious violence anything comes close to the slaughter of millions upon millions of victims by recent atheistic dictatorships.

In any case, denying the existence of immortal souls in the name of science certainly does nothing to protect people from being turned into valueless objects. So it is striking to us that a scattering of modern intellectuals, including scientific naturalists and now the New Atheists, have so confidently dismissed in the name of science what most of their fellow humans have believed since the birth of consciousness on Earth. For people of faith science has little or nothing to contribute to the question of an afterlife. Our expectation of life after death is open to neither scientific confirmation nor falsification.

Because hope for life beyond death is tied so closely to faith in God it is completely off limits to scientific examination. If God is trustworthy, as people of faith have always believed, then God will not abandon us to death. Because science and faith are independent of each other, even scientific studies of "near-death experiences" and other extraordinary psychological phenomena make no difference at all to those of us who take the contrast approach. It also goes without saying that belief in the resurrection of the body, like belief in the immortality of the soul, is a matter of faith and hope, not scientific discovery.

Expectation of life beyond death has been nearly universal since the dawn of human consciousness, and it is beyond the reach of science to decide whether this common belief is justified. Hindus and Buddhists also deny that death is the end of life altogether. They believe in reincarnation culminating in final liberation from the cycle of rebirths, so they too would reject scientific materialism's doctrine that mindlessness is the final destiny of all being. Even in the age of science, therefore, contrast takes seriously the testimony of most humans that our present existence is only a small patch in a much wider metaphysical setting. For most people who have ever lived, death is not the end of life. We strongly suspect that even hardcore materialists still rebel, at least at some level of their existence, against the notion that consciousness can ever be snuffed out completely.

Contrast, as you have by now come to understand, consistently claims that a sense of our connection to the eternal is hidden from minds that have not yet undergone the personal transformation and dramatic altering of worldview that faith requires. An authentic sense of the eternal is especially inaccessible to minds warped by scientism and conditioned to the shallows of mere spectator evidence. This is why some Christian theologians, for example, argue that the experience of Jesus's resurrection by his disciples would not have been accessible to cameras and scientific experimenters. To grasp the reality of such a momentous, world-shaking event one must undergo the radical shift of horizons that we call the "journey of faith." The same applies to any serious affirmation of immortality.

Today, we must admit, many educated people are simply not interested in the question of life after death. They are attracted to the scientific naturalist claim that nature is all there is and that no place exists for any imaginable state of immortality. However, we have noticed that there are different kinds of naturalists. Some are sunny and optimistic while others are sober and pessimistic. Sunny naturalists are those who find sufficient spiritual fulfillment here and now in the enjoyment of nature's beauty, human inquiry, and creativity. For them nature is enough to fill a person's life with meaning. Many scientists are sunny naturalists, professing to be fully satisfied with a life devoted to the adventure of discovery. To them the idea of a life beyond death has little appeal.[5]

Sober naturalists, on the other hand, are chronically unsatisfied. The thought saddens them that every life ends in death and that human consciousness and all its accomplishments will eventually lapse into irreversible mindlessness. They are deeply disappointed that nature is not resourceful enough to satisfy their longing for everlasting meaning, immortality, and happiness. Sober naturalists include good scientists who are honest enough to admit that they too have religious longings. Yet their allegiance to scientism frustrates any hope that death is not the end of them. For them nature is *not* enough to fill their restless human hearts with meaning and joy. And yet the idea of life after death seems to them to be only wishful thinking.

Contrast takes the sober naturalists seriously. Unlike the sunnier type, sober naturalists are clearheaded enough to acknowledge the ultimate futility of a life that ends in death without hope of redemption. The French writer Albert Camus (1913–60) speaks eloquently for sober naturalism when he freely confesses his own appetite for ultimate meaning and eternal life. It is dishonest, he says, to deny that we each have a longing for immortality and infinite happiness. However, Camus goes on to say that we have to admit that the natural world, no matter how expansive and lovely it may be, can never satisfy our longing for the eternal. If death is the decisive end of life, and mindlessness the ultimate destiny of nature's adventure in consciousness, then reality makes no sense in the final analysis. The idea that lovers of life find themselves in a death-dealing universe is the very definition of what Camus calls the "Absurd." Realistically, Camus concludes, no hope can ever surmount this impossible situation. Hence the hero of the human condition is Sisyphus, the exemplar of all striving in the face of futility.[6]

A more scientific spokesperson for sober naturalism is Steven Weinberg. This Nobel Prize-winning physicist at the University of Texas is thoughtful enough to acknowledge his own aspirations for indestructible meaning, but he claims that science shows our predicament to be hopeless:

> It would be wonderful to find in the laws of nature a plan prepared by a concerned creator in which human beings played some special role. I find sadness in doubting that we will. There are some among my scientific colleagues who say that the contemplation of nature gives them all the spiritual satisfaction that others have found in a belief in an interested God. Some of them may even feel that way. I do not.[7]

Like Camus, Weinberg takes seriously the question of God and human destiny, but he remains a partisan of scientism. Science, he believes, has exposed the impersonality of the universe, the finality of death, and the ultimate futility of life. Like Einstein, Weinberg thinks that science rules out the existence of a creator interested in our own individual lives. The only serious benefit we can reap from reflection on our lives, therefore, is a sense of honor at facing up to the tragedy of it all.[8]

Those of us who represent the contrast position respect Weinberg's repudiation of sunny naturalism. We agree with him and Camus that it would be dishonest not to acknowledge the pointlessness of any universe in which death is the end of everything. So if you are attracted to scientific naturalism at all, logic should lead you to side with the sober rather than the sunny version. Sober naturalism, as our earlier citation of William James also makes clear, faces more honestly what naturalism really entails. The finality of death, if death is the end, makes your life ultimately meaningless. If you had to make a choice, therefore, reason should force you to choose the tragic realism of Camus and Weinberg and avoid the sprightly romanticism of Flanagan and other sunny naturalists. Fortunately, as contrast argues throughout this book, you have a reasonable alternative to both sober and sunny naturalism. You may choose the path of faith.

Let us suppose for a moment, however, that you take either sober or sunny naturalism as your life's orientation. In either case, as the philosopher John Hick observes, you still have to face the fact that naturalism "is very bad news for humanity as a whole."[9] Maybe you live in a peaceful time and a prosperous place where you think you can find sufficient satisfaction in a naturalist pseudo-paradise. However, the pain, poverty, and unbearable suffering of most people locked outside your garden make it impossible for them to find fulfillment within the limits of nature alone. And what about you? Even if you live a long and productive life, as Hick adds, it is doubtful that before you die you will have completely fulfilled your potential. So if you are a naturalist of any stripe, you are refusing to face the facts if you fail to see that "naturalism is not good news for much of humanity."[10]

Faith, however, instructs us that there is an abiding and much more "real" world beneath, beyond, and behind the transient flow of events and individual lives.[11] Science is incapable of putting us in touch with this deeper dimension of reality, but for people of faith the passage of time and the perpetual perishing of events in the visible cosmos are merely a veil. Behind the veil there exists the timeless splendor of eternity. Time leads to death and loss, but faith points to a realm of permanence beyond time and becoming. The life of faith teaches us how to conquer the perishing of every moment in time by stretching our souls even now toward the infinite and eternal God who is our ultimate destiny.

CONVERGENCE

Human reflection on death has generally taken three distinct forms that parallel, respectively, conflict, contrast, and convergence. Without getting too technical, let us call these three views of human destiny "naturalistic fatalism," "otherworldly optimism," and "long-suffering hope." Henceforth we shall refer to these as "fatalism," "optimism," and "hope." *Fatalism* views all loss as permanent and irredeemable. It assumes that the stream of time and perishing events heads only toward complete nothingness, and that the universe is ultimately "pointless." Fatalism implies also that human life has no lasting purpose, although it allows for moments of satisfaction, including the occasional rush of courage in facing up to the reality of death. This is the conflict perspective.

Optimism is an approach to death that most people of faith still find attractive. It trusts that our destiny lies in a God who lives in an eternal present outside of time. Today those who embrace the otherworldly optimist's response to the world's perpetual perishing are often scientifically informed, but they generally consider modern science, including evolution, to be religiously inconsequential. Optimism holds that because science is concerned only with the temporal world, its discoveries, including ideas made famous by Darwin and Einstein, have no bearing on the religious sense of a timeless destiny awaiting us in an eternal present beyond all appearances. This is the approach that contrast generally follows.

Hope, our third option, acknowledges the fact of perpetual perishing, but it rejects both cosmic pessimism and the world escapism that accompanies otherworldly optimism. Hope interprets the irreversible flow of time as leading the whole universe, and not just individual human souls, forward, toward an everlasting fulfillment in the mystery of God. Hope takes seriously the new cosmic story laid open by the natural sciences. Hope understands our individual longing for the eternal to be inseparable from the larger question of what eventually happens to the whole universe. Our own destiny is inseparable from that of the cosmos. This is the convergence option.

Fatalism despairs of any ultimate meaning for both the universe and human beings. Optimism looks only for the survival of the human soul, or the personal "self," and cares little or nothing about what happens to the physical universe. Hope, however, is concerned about what happens to the entire course of events that make up the universe. This includes the pre-living natural world, the birth and evolution of life, the courses of billions of stars and galaxies, and all of human history. The question of an individual life's meaning goes hand in hand with the question of the ultimate meaning and destiny of the cosmic story.

141

Hope does not try to neutralize, reverse, or conquer time. Instead, it pictures the vast temporal, narrative unfolding of the universe as an adventurous journey of all creation into God in whose everlasting love it is saved from absolute loss. Hope views the universe as a story that truly matters to God and that contributes something everlasting to the life of God. And even if the physical universe (or multiverse) eventually undergoes "death" by energy exhaustion, to people of hope the story of its having been—along with all individual stories—will still be taken up forever into the life and compassion of God.

There can be no purely scientific evidence of this outcome, of course, but hope is consistent with the fact that throughout cosmic history so far something new and momentous has always been taking shape up ahead. Science, as we have seen, has demonstrated that the universe is still coming into being. Accordingly, hope views the universe not as perfect, but as a drama full of promise. Unlike otherworldly optimism, hope invites us to be fully involved here and now in the drama of transformation that we call the universe.

Hope, therefore, does not negate time or flee from the human task of contributing to the ongoing creation of the universe. As we emphasized earlier, our personal contribution to the great work of creation may consist of doing very mundane and monotonous things, but with a sense that our small efforts matter ultimately. From the perspective of hope, each passing moment is pregnant with an unprecedented future. What is permanent for hope is not an eternal divine stillness lurking above time but the newness of being that rises perpetually on the horizon of the future. Hope experiences the divine eternity through anticipation rather than comprehension. The passing of each moment is not simply loss to which we must fatalistically resign ourselves, but an opening to a continually new future. When we read in the Book of Isaiah (43:19) that God is "about to do a new thing," we think this applies to the whole universe as well as to human existence.

As the future arrives afresh in each moment, the newness of being that it brings with it pushes the present into the past. Nevertheless, this past still lives on in some way. It enters causally into the shaping of each new moment. Hope is not only a steady, wayfaring openness to what is new. It is also a refusal to consign the past to complete oblivion or meaninglessness. Hope looks toward a future redemption of all events, including those that have faded into the past. The redemptive future will in some way preserve and bring narrative coherence to the past by situating it in an ever-widening pattern of beauty.[12]

Fatalism, optimism, and hope all have ancient pedigrees. Fatalism's remote exemplar is ancient Greek tragedy and Stoicism. Optimism is foreshadowed by Plato's philosophy, with its emphasis on an unchanging ideal world existing above time, untouched by perishing. Hope finds its classic expression in the prophetic faith traditions that have understood time, in all of its transience, to be filled with the promise of a fulfillment beyond our reach. Convergence, which has its religious roots in Abrahamic hope, understands eternity as the fullness of time rather than as an unchanging completeness existing serenely apart from the flow of perishable events.

What choice will you make: fatalism, optimism, or hope? Realistically speaking, most of us create hybrid versions of the three options. Strands of fatalism, optimism, and hope often weave in and out in an individual's life, along with some degree of escapism. Fatalism is often tinged with optimism, optimism laced with hope, and hope never completely cured of impatience. Moreover, during the course of a single life one may oscillate back and forth along the range of options.

Nevertheless, where real life is tolerant of such ambiguity, theology seeks logical consistency. The three options cannot all be right. One of them—if indeed these are the only available options—must be more in tune with the nature of things, including what science has discovered, than are the others. Does science match up best with fatalism, optimism, or hope?

Let us at least set the stage for your own response. Logically speaking, you must first choose between fatalism on the one hand and optimism or hope on the other. That is, you must decide whether perishing is final or in some way redeemable. However, the option for immortality forks off into either optimism or hope. Otherworldly optimism tries to lift the shroud of impermanence abruptly and expose the divine eternity that allegedly lies beyond nature and human existence. Optimism, endorsed by contrast, looks behind the veil of becoming and perishing to a realm of unchanging being, goodness, and beauty. For Flanagan and his philosophical friends supernaturalist optimism is the only alternative to their naturalistic fatalism.

Convergence, however, argues that another religious option is available: the series of perishable cosmic, biological, and historical events is *itself* the path to the eternal, not an obstacle on that path. The cosmic story is a stream into whose current we may willingly immerse ourselves here and now. Hope's intuition is that the eternal lies not so much beneath or behind the passing flux of immediate things as up ahead, in the future. God is the goal of the whole universe's temporal passage. Both optimism and hope draw us toward the eternal, but optimism pulls us away from the universe. Hope, however, wagers that the whole current of perishable cosmic events flows into that which abides without end. For hope, the stream of cosmic becoming is not something to leap out of, but to dip into more fully and trustingly than either fatalism or optimism allows.

Optimism (contrast) is a kind of religious impatience. It is seductive because it speaks directly to our longing for permanence. It holds that an essential part of us, the soul, already stands partly outside of nature. Accordingly it views the physical universe as ultimately insignificant except as a context for soul making. Its greatest appeal lies in its belief that after death the soul can soar abruptly into a heavenly beyond. Unfortunately it dismisses our souls or selves from the Earth without letting us first taste fully of the fact of becoming and cosmic creativity. As theologian Reinhold Niebuhr puts it, optimism (which he calls "mysticism") has a "tendency to flee the responsibilities of history and engage in premature adventures into eternity."[13]

Ironically, then, optimism is a kind of cosmic pessimism in the sense that it gives up on the universe too soon. Optimism often implies that there is only a utilitarian value to the transient world and its evolution. That is, the universe exists primarily as a school in which persons may prepare for an eternity outside of time. Contrast and its brand of optimism fail to appreciate the narrative depth of the recently revealed 14 billion year cosmic story in which the human species has only lately arrived. The cosmic story remains only incidental to optimism's impatience. The otherworldly optimist springs cleanly out of this imperfect, unfinished—and hence ambiguous—universe, refusing to watch it unfold at its own pace, along an indeterminate and richly creative itinerary.

Hope, then, fosters a posture of patient, wayfaring cosmic expectation. It shares with optimism an intuition of the permanence beyond all change. However, it strives toward communion with God not by decisively rocketing out of the cosmic flux, but by staying patiently with the flow of events that carry an entire universe, and humans along with it, into an unimaginable future fulfillment. This patience is not passive but active, participating enthusiastically in the ongoing creation of the universe. What remains permanent for hope is not a realm of static perfection untouched by time, but an ever fresh future that draws into itself the continual flow of time. Hope does not seek to escape the world in order to find salvation. Instead it looks for the coming of God to a renewed Earth and still unfinished universe.

God, as theologian Karl Rahner puts it, is the Absolute Future. Beyond all relative futures, which will themselves eventually prove to be perishable, hope anticipates a future that brings the whole stream of events to fulfillment. According to hope's reading of transience in the universe, impermanent things are not illusions to be discounted, but *promises* that already bear within themselves, in an anticipatory way, the Absolute Future that is always coming and has not yet fully arrived. Convergence defends this hope as completely compatible with both faith and science.

Unlike Flanagan's fatalism, hope trusts that the entire universe has a purpose, or narrative coherence, that is hidden from view here and now. Hope provides a much less selective and arbitrary reading of the data of current natural science than that given by the alleged "realism" of cosmic pessimism. Hope and promise, we submit, are notions logically compatible with the ambiguity, incompleteness, and uncertainty of the present universe. It is hope, not cosmic pessimism or optimistic escapism, that matches up most naturally with the cosmic drama that science is now unveiling.

Finally, during our presentation, you may have been wondering about your personal, subjective immortality. What will happen to you? If here and now your mental life is dependent upon cellular, chemical, and physical processes, how can it survive the dissolution of death? Don't you have to go back to the optimist option to salvage any prospect of your subjective survival after death?

Not necessarily. Any possible survival of subjective identity beyond death has to mean, at the very least, that the entire story of our lives is taken into God and preserved everlastingly. This is the meaning of resurrection. Each personal self is built up over a lifetime by a unique series of interrelated events. Each life is an unrepeatable story of struggle, striving, enjoyment, anticipation, achievement, and failure. To give continuity and pattern to this series of events, each subjective center registers and to some degree preserves and holds its particular series of experiences in memory and anticipation. Apart from some degree of memory and anticipation, there can be no sense of subjective identity.

However, no mortal subject can remember forever every event that makes up its life story. And no mortal subject can ever clearly anticipate its destiny. Disease, accidents, old age, senility, and finally death dissolve each subjective center of experience and striving. For the fatalist this dissolution is final. For the optimist it is illusory. But for those who choose the path of hope, the story of each subject's life and experience is inseparable from the whole cosmic journey into God.

Hope trusts that every event that makes up the cosmic drama is taken into the divine life immediately, everlastingly, and without fading. This is the ageless message of our psalmists and prophets. God experiences everything faithfully and forever. To finite subjects every event fades into the past, and this is why we fear that we will be forgotten. But to God nothing is ever blotted out. Nothing ever fades into oblivion. In an age of science this means that the cosmos can really be called a story or drama only if there is an everlasting subject that experiences it without any diminishment of feeling, a subject that saves the universe in every detail and anticipates its ultimate destiny. This, at the very least, is what we mean by our idea of a "living God."

Convergence holds, therefore, that our own subjective survival is inseparable from the destiny of the whole series of events that we call the universe. If the whole cosmic drama has its destiny in God, so also do our own personal stories. Our hope is that these too will be patterned anew in the context of the larger story of creation. And it is inconceivable to us that a genuine resurrection would fail to reestablish our own subjective consciousness, although in a way that gives us a wider and deeper awareness of our intimate relationship to all of being.[14] The way to prepare for death, therefore, is to cultivate and intensify our relationship to the whole of cosmic reality here and now, becoming especially sensitive to the stories of other striving, struggling subjects.

However, to go just one step further, why should we suppose that God could transform and reconstitute only human narratives and not just as readily the stories of all living subjects? Any other God would be too small for us. The hope underlying convergence boldly suggests that not only human organisms but also the whole evolutionary drama of life, indeed the entire universe and, if relevant, the multiverse, may pass into the divine mystery and be "reincarnated" everlastingly in a transforming drama of unimaginable depth, breadth, and beauty. In the age of science any lesser prospect would be disheartening. Indeed, if we accept the new scientific intuition that our own existence is intricately woven into the tapestry of the whole of creation, how can we ever again separate our own expectation of a transforming personal resurrection from the destiny of the whole universe in the saving care and compassion of God?

CHAPTER 11

Does the Universe
Have a Purpose?

CONFLICT

No! Nothing in the natural sciences provides even a hint that the universe has any purpose. To say that something has a purpose means that it is moving toward a goal, but there is no evidence that our 14 billion-year-old universe is headed anywhere except to eventual extinction. Everything we have said in the preceding chapters leads to this conclusion. Even if the universe lasts for a trillion more years, it is hurling not toward a goal but only toward an ending, a final state of lifelessness. Death by energy exhaustion awaits everything.

Theists, following the ancient philosopher Aristotle and the faith assumptions of Jews, Christians, and Muslims, still believe in cosmic purpose. But scientific method has dropped the Aristotelian and theological concern about "why" things happen and is interested only in "how" things happen. Classical physics, starting with Galileo and Newton, emancipated our minds from suffocation by the religious obsession with purpose. Purpose, as Francis Bacon (1561–1626) pointed out in the early seventeenth century, doesn't explain anything. Only after natural philosophy abandoned the medieval concern with "teleology" (*telos* is the Greek word for goal) did the physical sciences really take off. Only after Darwin's notion of natural selection did away with the idea that life has a purpose, and after scientists showed that life could be explained in terms of chemistry, did biology finally become fully scientific.

As far as conflict is concerned, not only science but also philosophy and intellectual life in general need to be purified of preoccupation with teleology. The expulsion of purpose from enlightened human thought today applies as much to cosmology—the study of the universe—as to physics and biology. If science lets even a whiff of teleology affect its ideas, it will compromise its integrity. Science is committed to a materialist worldview and materialism implies purposelessness. The Harvard biologist Richard Lewontin forcefully and faithfully represents the conflict position. He admits that common sense cannot avoid talking about purposes. For example, right now you are reading this page with the purpose of understanding it. But science is not common sense. It is not interested in purpose. Look carefully at Lewontin's remarks:

> Our willingness to accept scientific claims that are against common sense is the key to an understanding of the real struggle between science and the supernatural. We take the side of science...because we have a prior commitment, a commitment to materialism. It is not that the methods and institutions of science somehow compel us to accept a material explanation of the phenomenal world, but, on the contrary, that we are forced by our a priori adherence to material causes to create an apparatus of investigation and a set of concepts that produce material explanations, no matter how counterintuitive, no matter how mystifying to the uninitiated. Moreover, that materialism is absolute, for we cannot allow a Divine Foot in the door.[1]

By embracing materialist naturalism we are free to forget about purpose and instead concentrate on digging back into the cosmic past and tracing the chains of physical causes that led up to present-day realities. This is the only reliable way to explain anything. Looking for purpose in nature is a distraction from the task of truly explaining things. We just stick to the observable data and avoid wild guesses about the meaning of it all. Our impartial examination of empirical data leads us straight to cosmic pessimism, the conviction that the universe as a whole lacks any purpose. We are aware, of course, that humans are meaning-seeking beings. In the commonsense world we do set goals for ourselves. But that doesn't mean that the universe is teleological.

Some years ago, in the midst of a highly acclaimed career in physics, Steven Weinberg wrote that as the universe has become more and more comprehensible to science the more "pointless" it now seems.[2] Our conflict approach completely agrees with Weinberg. It disturbs us that some physicists—for example, John Polkinghorne, Freeman Dyson, and Paul Davies are still open to the idea of cosmic purpose.[3] However, there is not enough evidence to support their flirtation with theology. The Cornell professor of natural history, William Provine, is perfectly justified in saying that

> modern science directly implies that the world is organized strictly in accordance with mechanistic principles. There are no purposive principles whatsoever in nature. There are no gods and no designing forces that are rationally detectable. The frequently made assertion that modern biology and the assumptions of the Judeo-Christian tradition are fully compatible is false.[4]

What, then, does this severe cosmic pessimism mean for you personally? In 1948 the renowned physicist James Jeans gave a colorful rendition of this question:

> Is this, then, all that life amounts to—to stumble, almost by mistake, into a universe which was clearly not designed for life, and which, to all appearances, is either totally indifferent or definitely hostile to it, to stay clinging on to a fragment of a grain of sand until we are frozen off, to strut on our tiny stage with the knowledge that our aspirations are all but doomed to final frustration, and that our achievements must perish with our race, leaving the universe as though we had never been?[5]

Our answer is "yes." However, we hasten to add that this response should not sadden you. Rather, it should uplift you. It means that you can now create your own meanings. So get busy, create your own meanings, and stop grumbling about the "pointlessness" of the universe. The late paleontologist Stephen Jay Gould got it right when he said that if you can't find any purpose in nature it only means that you will have to define meaning for yourself. So the absence of cosmic purpose is not a misfortune but an opportunity.[6] The meaningless universe is a blank slate upon which you may now inscribe your own values and goals. You don't have to follow some eternal script devised by a divine designer.

The American philosopher E. D. Klemke also finds a meaning-less universe more than acceptable:

> From the standpoint of present evidence, evaluational com-ponents such as meaning or purpose are not to be found in the universe as objective aspects of it....Rather, we "impose" such values upon the universe....An objective meaning—that is, one which is inherent within the universe or dependent upon external agencies—would, frankly, leave me cold. It would not be mine....I, for one, am glad that the universe has no mean-ing, for thereby is man all the more glorious. I willingly accept the fact that external meaning is non-existent,...this leaves me free to forge my own meanings.[7]

CONTRAST

Cosmic pessimism is inseparable from the materialist worldview embraced by conflict. Scientism and scientific materialism lead natu-rally to the denial of cosmic purpose. At the roots of cosmic pessimism lies a belief that the only evidence that counts is scientific evidence. It logically follows from scientism and materialism that nature is all there is. If so, the cosmos is pointless, as Weinberg claims.

However, once again, contrast's reply is that, strictly speaking, scientism and scientific materialism are beliefs and not insights gained from scientific investigation or experimentation. No scientific experi-ments have ever demonstrated that matter is all there is or that the uni-verse is pointless. So cosmic pessimism is no less rooted in belief than is teleology or theology. Cosmic pessimism is the result of confusing science with tragic and fatalistic suppositions that have nothing to do with scientific inquiry. If you already believe the universe is nothing more than a physical system—as Lewontin admits to doing—then obviously the universe will strike you as pointless. But science itself does not require that you become a cosmic pessimist.

Contrast agrees that scientific method itself is not interested in finding purpose in the universe. It is not part of scientific method either to affirm or deny that the cosmos is teleological. So science should not be forced to answer a question for which it is naturally unqualified. Cosmic pessimism is not science but a worldview that gives a negative answer to the perennial human question about whether there is an inherent meaning to the universe. People become cosmic pessimists for all sorts of nonscientific reasons, and these extraneous motivational factors may be purely temperamental, cultural, or philosophical. Look closely for example, at Lewontin's words cited approvingly by conflict earlier in this chapter. This highly respected intellectual clearly admits that it is not scientific investigation but his prior philosophical belief in materialism that rules out any theological understanding of nature.

If science cannot find any purpose in the universe, however, is theology able to do so? Not really. Although we believe in God, those of us who take the contrast approach doubt whether faith and theology can say much about cosmic purpose either. Neither science nor theology can clarify what the universe is really all about. Such matters are shrouded in mystery. Faith trusts that there is a purpose to everything, but it is blind as to what this purpose might be.

We admire all the scientists, therefore, who seek to purify science of any concern with God or purpose. Good science always brackets out the biggest questions people ask. Science's avoidance of teleology is not a defect but a strength. At the same time, we believe good theology should also remain silent on the question of cosmic purpose. Isn't it sufficient that faith gives meaning to our personal lives? Why should we worry about cosmic destiny? Such a question is too big for us, anyway. It is also too big for scientists. When scientists like Weinberg become cosmic pessimists, they want us to assume that their judgments about the indifference of the world come directly from science. But science is not equipped to dish out any such information. Nor are theologians in a position to tell us what the "point" of the universe might be.

Genuine faith and theology, after all, have an "apophatic" aspect. That is, they make a place for silence. Silence in the life of faith is the way in which we confess the inadequacy of our understanding of God and what God may be doing in the universe. The more important our questions are, the less clear will be the answers to them. Certitude is always out of place in matters of faith. Faith, as we have said before, is not a kind of grasping but a stance of "being grasped by" that which is of ultimate importance. This is why science will never find God. And this is also why theology won't either. Faith is a matter not of finding but of allowing ourselves to be found. The practice of silence in prayer is one important way in which we admit the limitations of even our most important symbols and names for God. Any confident claims by theologians about the meaning or purpose of the universe need to be taken with a big grain of salt.

The humility of authentic scientific research corresponds nicely with faith's own proper sense of the limits of human knowing. By entrusting to God's mysterious providence and wisdom the answers to our biggest questions, the human mind is liberated to focus day by day on issues more proportionate to our human limitations. Faith allows those of us who are scientists to relax into our scientific pursuits because it instructs us that the big issues—such as cosmic purpose— need not become our concern. The wisdom of our faith traditions cautions us that it is not our business to know the purpose of the universe. Here we take our lead from the Book of Job:

> Then the LORD answered Job out of
>   the whirlwind:
> "Who is this that darkens counsel by
>   words without knowledge?
> Gird up your loins like a man,
>   I will question you, and you shall
>   declare to me.

"Where were you when I laid the
  foundation of the earth?
Tell me, if you have understanding. (Job 38:1–4)

Finally, contrast is appalled by the suggestions of Gould and Klemke that a pointless universe is an opportunity for each of us to create our own meanings. Nothing could be sillier or more dangerous. If we were the sole creators of our own values, meanings, and goals, what is to prevent us from making self-aggrandizement or world domination the purpose of our lives? To contrast, purpose is not something we invent but instead something to which we can only respond. The meaning of our lives is not to create values, but to allow ourselves to be grasped and challenged by them. This is why we suggest that faith—the state of being "swept away" by an infinite goodness, beauty, and truth—is the surest way to find meaning.

CONVERGENCE

We cannot expect to understand what's really going on in the universe without taking into account what the natural sciences are telling us about it. And even though scientific method is not directly interested in purpose, we cannot help reflecting on the possible significance of scientific *discoveries*. Don't the findings of geology, biology, and cosmology have some relevance to the question of cosmic purpose?

But what do we mean by purpose? *Purpose* means quite simply being oriented toward what is self-evidently good. To have purpose, a set of events must be in the process of realizing something of value. For example, our own lives have purpose if we experience them as contributing to values or causes that will outlast us. Convergence thinks of the universe itself as a series of events in which something of great significance is working itself out. But what could this possibly be?

It could be named in many ways, but let's start with the undeniable fact that the universe has lately given birth to intelligence. That the universe has produced something so exquisitely sublime as your own mind should make you pause before declaring, along with cosmic pessimists, that our mind-making cosmos is evidently pointless. As you saw in chapter 9, the physics of the early universe can no longer be understood independently of the phenomena of life and mind. Scientists are increasingly willing to admit that we live in an essentially mind-making universe and that the emergence of mind in the Big Bang universe is no mere coincidence.

Cosmic pessimists, however, feel obliged to repudiate purpose at all costs. Since the Big Bang universe has always held the promise of bursting into mind, wouldn't that be enough to restrain us from declaring that the universe is pointless? "No," the cosmic pessimist replies. Mind or intelligence is a cosmic fluke that tells us nothing about the universe itself. In order to suppress the impression that a "mindful" universe may have a deep and lasting importance, the cosmic pessimists today often resort to the idea of an essentially mindless "multiverse." If our own mind-bearing universe is only one of countless universes, then it could have arisen by mere accident. By hypothesizing a multiverse the cosmic pessimist tries to recover the requisite flukiness needed to restore pointlessness to the whole scheme of things.

Intelligence, however, is itself thoroughly purposeful. *Purpose* means "striving toward a goal," and the mind's performance is the best and most immediate example we have of striving to realize a goal. Even the cosmic pessimist's mind cannot exist or function without having goals that keep it churning. The scientific materialist's own mind cannot help seeking the self-evident values of intelligibility and truth. Your own mind too is activated because you *value* meaning and truth. In reading this chapter at this very moment you are striving to reach the goal of understanding. You are trying to understand the meaning of the words on this page, and you are also asking if the various claims made in this book are true. This is because you value truth as one of the goals of intelligent inquiry. So the evidence of your own mind's purposiveness is right there in front of you. You can have no reasonable doubt that purposeful striving for understanding and truth is going on in your mind. The same kind of striving for intelligibility and truth is even going on in the cosmic pessimist's mind.

But does the fact that your mind is now striving to reach the goals of intelligibility and truth mean that the universe has a purpose? It does if there is a sufficiently tight connection between your mind and the physical universe. But is there a tight connection? Cosmic pessimism, which is a major component of conflict's worldview, denies that there is. Cosmic pessimism is based on the tacit assumption that mind and nature are separate and essentially unrelated. The early modern dualism of mind and matter is still around, encouraging the cosmic pessimist to claim that the purposeful striving of the human mind has no implications whatsoever for how to understand nature. The contrast position likewise assumes a parallel divide between nature and the human person. Conflict and contrast, far apart though they may seem to be, share the assumption that mind or subjectivity is not really part of the natural world. This dualistic presupposition is what allows conflict to declare that nature is essentially mindless, and the same persistent dualism permits contrast to dismiss scientific discoveries about the physical universe as theologically irrelevant.

Convergence, on the other hand, emphasizes the narrative connection of your mind to the physics of the cosmos. Since the universe now shows itself to be a story, we look for its meaning not only by breaking its complex evolutionary outcomes down into elemental units but, as we stated in chapter 9, by looking to the future for a narrative coherence that may tie everything together up ahead. We are interested in reading the universe as a series of events, episodes, and epochs in a single, still unfolding story. If we read the universe in this narrative way, the physical events that occurred in the early chapters of cosmic history cannot be divorced from the purposefulness now on display in your own mind's striving to reach understanding and truth. Nature and mind are aspects of one big story. It has taken 14 billion years for the cosmic drama to ripen to the point of blossoming into minds, but at least a loose directionality has been there all along.

And if it takes a multiverse to make one mind-bearing universe, then the story may be larger than expected, but there would still be a narrative connection between your mind and the hypothetical totality of worlds. As we have noted on several occasions, to have a story you need a blend of accidents, "lawfulness," and duration. A multiverse would also have a narrative constitution. It would consist of the three ingredients that make stories possible: enormously large numbers, a lawful pruning or sifting of probabilities by a principle of selection, and an unimaginable sequence of epochs. A multiverse would possess, in other words, the three components that would still allow it to have a narrative intelligibility that could conceivably carry a purpose. The universe (or multiverse) has always held the promise of becoming intelligent. Consequently, convergence claims that the obvious purposefulness of your mind, as it reaches out for deeper intelligibility and truth, is in a very real sense *the cosmos itself* reaching out (through your mind) toward these same goals. Any other conclusion would take you back to the obsolete dualistic illusion that your mind is not really part of the universe.

We can now picture our conflict adversaries reacting to what we have just said. Their own minds are busy looking around for reasons to refute the convergence position. Yet in their search for reasons to refute us their minds have the goal of finding intelligibility and truth. Cosmic pessimists clearly show that they too trust the capacity of their own minds to reach these exquisite goals. All you have to do is read books by the likes of Richard Dawkins, Daniel Dennett, and Jerry Coyne to sense the enormous degree of confidence they have in their own cognitional performance. And yet, if the universe that gave birth to their minds is essentially mindless (and hence pointless), as they claim, then they have no good reason to trust these same minds.

Our response to this self-contradiction is to take contemporary science more seriously and consistently than scientific skeptics and cosmic pessimists do. To us science has now demonstrated that the physical universe and human intelligence are inseparable dimensions of a single cosmic drama. Nothing that happened in the cosmos prior to the recent evolutionary arrival of goal-oriented human persons can be separated from our own striving. There is a narrative coherence that ties matter inextricably to the drama of our own intellectual striving. Through our own anticipation of meaning and truth the whole anticipatory universe reaches out implicitly toward everlasting values.

There is no purpose, after all, apart from striving. With the emergence of life, striving toward goals first came into the cosmos 4 billion years ago. Once again, it is the fact of striving toward goals that allows us to distinguish what is alive from what is not. With the gradual complexification of nervous systems came sentience, the capacity to register feelings and to strive more energetically. Subjective centers of feeling and striving continued to complexify in evolution. Eventually animals appeared, and life became increasingly prone to strive and struggle.

It was into this long story of striving toward goals that eventually human intelligence appeared. And then, for the first time, the universe awakened to the conscious pursuit of purpose. Minds emerged, and the universe began intentionally to pursue goals. What goals? Humans strive not only for pleasure but also for happiness. The pursuit of happiness, however, requires as its necessary condition the pursuit of goals that we call values. Happiness, then, is not the same as pleasure. Although the two can go together at times, happiness can be experienced even in the midst of suffering and in the absence of sensual satisfaction. The pursuit of pleasure can bring temporary satisfaction, but happiness can outlast pleasure because it is based on a sense of being grasped by everlasting values that endure even when everything else is lost. Devotion to permanent values is what gives humans a sense of meaning and hence happiness in their lives. Humans are animals whose very vitality depends on their being able to find meaning. It has been especially the function of our faith traditions to guarantee the everlastingness of the values whose pursuit gives meaning or purpose to our lives. Faith and theology refer to the eternal ground of values as "God."

What then are the values that give your own life meaning? You may answer this question by looking into your own inquiring mind in which the universe has now become conscious of itself in a uniquely personal way. Your best access to the mystery of the cosmos is to peer through the portals of your own consciousness and your own striving for meaning. You will find the answer to this chapter's question by examining the goals or values that bring you happiness. These goals are especially *meaning, truth, goodness,* and *beauty.* In giving birth to intelligence the universe has recently awakened explicitly to values that have been quietly hovering on the horizon at every stage of cosmic becoming. By reflecting on how the pursuit of these goals enlivens and illuminates your own life, you will have access to what it is that moves the universe as well.

You and the universe are a package deal. Science has demonstrated unmistakably that your intelligence is stitched seamlessly into the larger drama of life and the story of the universe. Nature has been ripening toward the eruption of mind since the first moments of cosmic history. The emergence and intensification of consciousness is not a local terrestrial accident, even if it turns out that our planet is the only place where life and mind have ever existed.[8] The root system of your consciousness is the entire universe and perhaps a multiverse, since the existence of only one life-bearing universe may somehow require the statistical immensity of innumerable worlds.

Our point is that the presence of intelligence in only one very local region or epoch of a multiverse still has a tight narrative connection to the larger panorama of worlds. Consider the fact that astronomers are right now extending their own minds out over a hypothesized plurality of universes so as to gather this enormity into an intelligible unity. This leap of the astrophysical mind in the direction of a multiverse is perfectly consistent with our vision of a world gradually awakening to infinite meaning, truth, goodness, and beauty, an awakening that can occasionally arouse the response of love. In our capacity for love, the cosmic story opens itself most fully to the infinite and eternal goodness it has been striving toward throughout the drama of life.

To cosmic pessimists, of course, it seems obvious that intelligent striving is an unintended accident simply because its emergence is apparently both late and local. However, even if intelligence is confined to the Earth and to a limited period of cosmic history, it does not follow that it has no narrative connection to the whole of things.[9]

Since the phenomenon of "thought" is intricately connected to the process of astronomical, terrestrial, and biological evolution, intelligence is an important key to understanding what the universe is really all about.

But is there purpose here? Yes. For any series of events to have purpose it must be oriented toward achieving something undeniably valuable. So inasmuch as the cosmic process gives birth to intelligence, and intelligence is awakened as a response to the undeniable values of meaning, truth, goodness, and beauty, the whole universe exhibits the character of being purposeful. Purpose in the universe, of course, means much more than the birth of consciousness, but any universe that has always held the promise of becoming intelligent can rightly be called purposeful.

Judaism, Christianity, and Islam all agree that the universe is here for a reason. They have different ways of expressing what this reason is, and, as contrast accurately indicates, they are cautious about expressing the fathomless ways of God. But convergence cannot separate our personal lives from the cosmic story that led to the capacity for faith and hope. Our lives are caught up with the whole universe in a mysterious movement toward infinite meaning, truth, beauty, love, new life, and communion with an eternal goodness. For Jews, the Sabbath itself is a foretaste of creation's final resting in God. For Christians, the eucharistic communion with Christ is a promise of final union of the whole universe with God. For Muslims, following the Five Pillars of faith, prayer, almsgiving, fasting, and pilgrimage is already to live in the presence of Allah, the merciful and compassionate source and destiny of all things.

The Abrahamic faiths stand or fall with the question of cosmic purpose. Today, as we have granted, considerable theological revision may be required to have a fruitful convergence of science with faith's sense of ultimate meaning. Such an undertaking is never finished, but we may begin the task by observing once again that science has gifted us with the picture of a universe still in the making. Our hope, therefore, need not be solely for our personal fulfillment but also for the cosmic process as a whole. We are not advocating here any new confusion or conflation of science with faith, nor do we wish to force the data of science into any preexisting theological schemes. Our claim is simply that science's sense of an unfinished universe provides an intelligible setting for the theme of *promise* that we have inherited from the Abrahamic faith traditions.

Science up until recently has focused on the "laws" of nature and failed to notice the universe's *dramatic* character. This oversight is significant, because as long as the universe is seen as essentially static and storyless it is difficult to think of it as having any possible point. However, because we now realize that the cosmos is an unfolding story, it is not unreasonable to ask what the meaning (or meanings) of the story might be. Nature, as we have noted before, points to an underlying narrative cosmological principle. The universe (or multiverse) is composed of the elements of chance, lawfulness, and deep time that make it a story worth reading at many levels. To convergence it is a story in which the promise of surprising outcomes has been present from the beginning.

Looking back, for example, at the cosmic story with a sensibility shaped by faith's participation in the story of our common father Abraham, we cannot help but see the whole cosmic story as the long unfolding of a promise. From the first moments of the cosmic dawn, for example, matter was already seeded with promise. It was prepared from the beginning to undergo transformations that created hydrogen atoms, galactic clusters, supernovas, carbon, organic molecules, life, and eventually intelligence. Imagine that you had been able to survey our universe shortly after the Big Bang. As you looked out over the featureless primordial plasma, or as you later inspected the endless expanse of hydrogen and helium atoms, could you ever have predicted that out of such a sea of monotony would eventually come life, mind, and the capacity for selfless love? Probably not. And yet the promise of such outcomes was present even in the midst of what would have seemed quite unpromising.

Nature, as it turns out, has always been pregnant with promise. It still is. Right now who of us is in a position to declare with confidence that the cosmos is completely pointless? Cosmic pessimism seems to convergence to be an arbitrary and unreasonable way to interpret the natural world. The new cosmic story does not allow you to separate your own purpose-driven mind neatly from the rest of the cosmos, as both conflict and contrast do. Your personal life and mind are so intricately intertwined with all of physical reality and the cosmic story that you cannot expect to understand who and what you are without asking what's going on in the universe.

Finally, however, for the cosmos to have a purpose, this purpose must be permanent. There must be something that saves the events, episodes, and epochs of the cosmic story from total death. This everlastingness is in part what the word God is pointing toward. God is the ground of the values that give purpose to the universe, but God also registers and saves everything that occurs in the story. Theologically speaking, the universe of contemporary science can have a purpose ultimately if it is a story that is always being woven into the eternal life of God.

CHAPTER 12

What If Extraterrestrials Exist?

CONFLICT

The discovery of extraterrestrial intelligence (ETI), should it ever occur, would mark the end of the Abrahamic faith traditions. The narrowly provincial God of Judaism, Christianity, and Islam would seem so small as to be unworthy of worship. If ETI exists, our own human sense of being exceptionally important in the universe would be ruined. The belief by Jews, Christians, and Muslims that they have been specially chosen by God would no longer make any sense. Intelligent beings from other planets in the universe could never understand terrestrial theological jargon. It is unlikely that extraterrestrials (ETs) would even ask the silly questions humans do about the meaning of life or the purpose of the universe. Thus there would be no need for religious illusions. The contemporary scientific search for extraterrestrial intelligence (SETI) can flourish best in the cultural atmosphere of scientific naturalism. There is a fundamental conflict between the adventurous spirit of SETI and the stay-at-home smugness of Abrahamic religious traditions.

CONTRAST

Theologians, contrary to what you have just heard from our conflict opponents, have long entertained the idea of the existence of extraterrestrial intelligent beings and "worlds." Such realms exist not only in "heaven" (the angelic hosts) but in "the heavens" as well.[1]

Indeed, some theologians even in the Middle Ages assumed that intelligent beings existed on the moon and many places in addition to Earth. Since we already believe that God has created spiritual beings other than humans, it would hardly be shocking to us if scientific explorers eventually find other intelligent beings in the physical universe. Consequently, it would not significantly alter our understanding of God's creativity, love, and providence if we find that ETI exists. To be frank, if SETI meets with success it will hardly make any difference to a faith and theology that are already tuned in to the infinite creative extravagance of God.

So contrast in no way rules out the existence of ETI. The existence of other "civilizations" in our Big Bang universe (or, if it exists, a multiverse) is completely consistent with the infinite and inexhaustible resourcefulness of the God of Abraham. Nevertheless, it is probably a waste of time even to speculate about an actual theological conversation between us and ETs. Given the enormous distances that separate our planet from any other possible intelligent civilizations, it is doubtful that much of an encounter is going to take place for a long time. And if and when it does, communication along the electromagnetic spectrum will be maddeningly slow. Even in the neighborhood of our own galaxy whole lifetimes would go by while initial greetings are being exchanged. So the topic of ETI seems an unnecessary distraction to theology as we understand it.

CONVERGENCE

The discovery of an extraterrestrial world of living and intelligent beings elsewhere in our universe would, to say the least, be a most interesting new stimulus to theology. Reflecting on even the remotest prospect of eventual "contact" with ETI—whether it ever occurs or not—is a wholesomely expansive exercise for theology. And it seems appropriate even now to respond to the claims the conflict position makes that contact with ETI would spell the end of faith and theology.

These are the relevant questions:

1. If we ever encounter ETI, what would happen to the notion of God?
2. Would our own sense of significance in the universe be diminished?
3. What would be the implications for the three Abrahamic traditions that identify themselves as specially chosen, as people set apart (the question of religious particularity)?
4. Would our own faith traditions and theologies make any sense to intelligent beings from other planets?
5. What implications would the discovery of other intelligent beings have on the large question of cosmic purpose?
6. And can faith and theology provide us with a conceptual framework that would be hospitable to, and perhaps even enthusiastic about, the prospect of meeting up with ETI?

We shall say only a few words about the first three of these questions and devote a bit more attention to the latter three.

What Would Happen to the *Notion* of God?

An encounter with alternative intelligent worlds would be yet another great occasion for theology to benefit from the discoveries of cosmology and enlarge its sense of God and divine creativity. But contact with ETI would also provide an opportunity for theology to display the unifying power of radical monotheism. Any intelligent communities in this universe outside of the Earth's would obviously be grounded in the same creative principle that our terrestrial monotheisms worship as the source of all things "visible and invisible." Our monotheism (belief in only one God) implies that all things, all forms of life, all peoples, and all worlds have a common origin and destiny in the one God who creates and encompasses all beings impartially.

Abrahamic monotheism is still the surest ground we have for embracing anything in creation that may at first seem alien to us.[2] To learn to love what God loves is the vocation and the constant struggle to which our prophets have already called us. Of course, tribalism and ethnic hatred, as well as disregard for nonhuman forms of life, still tragically persist here on Earth. However, this is so only because monotheism, which emphasizes the ontological unity underlying all diversity, still has too tenuous a hold on human awareness. Unfortunately, many people on our small planet do not yet *really* believe in the ultimate unity of all beings even here in our own world. The discovery of other intelligent worlds would be a powerful new incentive to radicalize monotheistic faith and confirm the fundamental unity of the cosmos.

Viewed theologically, all galaxies and all universes are rooted in an ultimate unity of being. So our space travels could never bring us into an encounter with anything completely alien to us. Theology's relevance to SETI lies most fundamentally in its conviction that all possible worlds have a common origin in the one God. And by virtue of the omnipresence of this one God, we too would have an extended home in all possible worlds to which we might eventually travel.[3]

Furthermore, we agree with contrast that the fundamental unity of all beings implied in the notion of divine creativity would tend, by its very nature, to unfold in an unlimited *diversity* of ways, and possibly a multitude of different "worlds" as implied by the idea of a multiverse. In the *Summa Theologica* Thomas Aquinas poses the childlike question as to why God created so many different kinds of beings. He answers that the endless multiplicity and diversity of creatures exist so that what is lacking in one thing as far as expressing the infinity of God is concerned can be supplied by something else, and what is lacking in the latter can be expressed by something else, and so on.[4] Diversity in creation, in other words, is appropriate precisely because of the nature of an infinitely resourceful creator. Our belief that the infinity of God has already become partially manifested in the extravagant multiplicity of nonliving and living beings on our own planet should already have prepared our minds and hearts for a disclosure of even richer diversity elsewhere—and in ways completely unfamiliar to us now. Perhaps there is no better way for religious people to prepare themselves for "exo-theology" than by developing here and now an "eco-theology" deeply appreciative of the revelatory richness of the variety of life forms on our planet.[5]

Would Our Own Sense of Significance Be Diminished?

Would knowledge of the existence of more intelligent and perhaps more ethically developed beings elsewhere undermine our self-esteem, thus making our faith traditions seem woefully provincial and unduly anthropocentric in convincing their devotees that they are somehow special? What would be the theological implications of an extended "Copernican Principle," one whereby Earth's intelligent occupants would be shown to be just one more "average" population in a universe comprising countless intelligent worlds?

In the first place, we can be confident that it is biologically inconceivable that there would be other *humans* anywhere else in the universe; so our uniqueness as a species is virtually guaranteed in any case. "Of men elsewhere, and beyond, there will be none forever," writes the evolutionist Loren Eiseley. Natural selection has brought *Homo sapiens* into the universe along genetically specific roads that will "never be retraced" biologically.[6]

Second, and more to the point, however, according to the great teachers of Islam, Judaism, and Christianity, we express our own unique human dignity and value not by looking for signs of our mental or ethical superiority over other forms of life but by following a path of service and even self-sacrifice with respect to the whole of life, wherever it may be present. Authentic existence, as Buddhism also makes clear, consists of our capacity for compassion rather than the urge toward competition. The meaning of our existence consists in part of the opportunity to donate our lives and moral efforts to something larger, more important and more enduring than ourselves. Thus, it is inconceivable that the eventual encounter with beings that may in some ways be our superiors would ever render such instruction obsolete.

What Would Be the Implications for the Abrahamic Traditions (the Question of Religious Particularity)?

Perhaps, though, contact with ETI would be the occasion of heightened anguish to those faiths that believe they have received special election and revelation from God. Wouldn't an encounter with other forms of personal, free, and responsible beings put considerable strain on the credibility of faith traditions that claim the status of being "a people set apart"?

The claim of special election might possibly undergo some stress after "contact." One response, of course, would be to treat ETs as potential subjects of conversion, in which case contact would simply provide new fields for missionary activity. Mary Russell conjures up such an approach—together with its potential hazards—in her interesting science fiction novel, *The Sparrow*.[7]

However, in the context of Abrahamic faith, the idea of special election is even now being divested of the connotations of rank and privilege that it might formerly have suggested. Election, the sense of being specially called or set apart by God, must be understood essentially as a vocation to serve the cause of life and justice rather than lifting us out of our fundamental relatedness to the entire cosmic community of beings. Christians, for example, will recall that Jesus's own sense of being called by God did not prevent him from taking on the status of a slave and of being subjected to the most humiliating destiny available during his lifetime, that of crucifixion (Phil 2). The God of justice espoused by the prophetic traditions requires a radical inclusiveness, a full embrace of the alien and marginalized. This inclusiveness would be open to ETs and supportive of the adventures of many intelligent worlds. Contact, once again, would require not an abandonment but instead a fuller appropriation of the central teachings and practice of the faith.

What seems to be universally applicable in the Abrahamic faith traditions is the ideal of hospitality, of embracing strangers, an ideal that beckons and challenges, no matter how much it has been ignored in practice. The history of our traditions is ambiguous at best in meeting this challenge, but historically the encounter of people of faith with those of alien cultures and practices has often led to the enrichment rather than the dissolution of their faith and theologies. Consequently we anticipate that in the far distant future, if interstellar travel ever occurs, contact with extraterrestrial "cultures" will provide fresh challenges and opportunities for growth.

Would Our Faith Traditions and Theologies Make Sense to Intelligent Beings from Other Planets?

This brings us, however, to a fourth and perhaps more interesting question for theology as it hypothetically prepares for contact. Would the "Others" (let us use this designation rather than "aliens") be able to make any sense at all of our own religious life and thought? And should we expect that other intelligent beings would practice anything like what we call religions? Let us put aside once again the sobering probability that, because of the enormous distances they would have to traverse, any messages flowing back and forth at the speed of light would not add up to many exchanges in the course of a single human lifetime, nor would they extend very far beyond our own cosmic neighborhood. For example, if you sent a message from one edge of the Milky Way galaxy to the other edge, it would take 200,000 years to get a reply. However, let us suppose that we shall eventually be given the opportunity of prolonged conversation with other beings who impress us as being both alive and intelligent. What must their own kind of life and intelligence be like in order to allow us to share with them in a meaningful way our own deepest hopes, including ideas about "God" or "salvation"? What are some of the marks that any other conceivable instances of intelligent life in this universe would have to possess in order for us to be able to converse with them about our own religious beliefs and that might also open us up to an understanding of theirs, if they have any?

In contemplating such questions we are reminded of just how much our earthly religions borrow, in the way of both content and expression, from the unique natural features of our own planet. We may assume that religions in other worlds would be idiosyncratically shaped by their own natural environments. Our own persistent religious metaphors are inseparable from the experience of *Earth's* own characteristics: rotation from day to night; the exposure to sun and moon; the existence of deserts, oceans, rivers and streams, clouds, rain, storms and whirlwinds, grass and trees, blood and breath, soil and sexuality, maternity, paternity, sisterhood and brotherhood. Think of how prominently our experience of trees, for example, shapes religious imagery: the tree of life, the tree of "knowledge of good and evil," the Bodhi tree of Buddha's enlightenment, the tree of the cross, the cedars of Lebanon. Think of how the occurrence of seeds sprouting to life out of Earth's topsoil has given us the highly significant religious metaphor of "resurrection." And the notion of "spirit," now ironically employed to refer to what is unearthly, comes from the Latin *spiritus* (in Hebrew *ruach* and in Greek *pneuma*), a notion that originally meant the "breath of life" and that, as we now realize, requires the existence of Earth's enlivening atmosphere as its physical basis. Imagine what our religions would be like, Thomas Berry asks, if we lived on something like a lunar landscape.[8] Wouldn't extraterrestrial ecologies breed other extraordinary blendings of land, life, and religious meaning? And wouldn't we have a very difficult time connecting with them?

Difficult, perhaps, though not impossible. Yet in order to conceive of how we might be able to engage in anything like theological conversation with cosmic Others we need first to clarify our terms. What exactly do we mean by *life*, by *intelligence*, and by *religion*?

First, *life*. As we observed in chapter 6, what allows us to identify living beings as "alive" at all, and thus lets us distinguish them from nonliving things or processes, is that they share with us humans the trait of *striving* to achieve some goal, and therefore the possibility of failing or succeeding.[9] We suggest, then, that human persons are interested in the possibility of life elsewhere in the universe in great measure because we sense that we share something special with all other striving, struggling beings. We feel a kinship with all other struggling beings who participate in the drama of life, a connection that we do not have with inanimate things. And so, if we ever encountered life on other worlds we would call it alive (regardless of its chemical makeup) only if we recognized that it participates with us in a kind of dramatic striving that risks the possibility of failure. Of course, in our search for life elsewhere we would also be on the lookout for such qualities as the transgenerational sharing of information that we find in the genetic flow of life here on Earth. We would look for open, self-organizing systems that pump energy out of their environment and so maintain themselves at a high level of complexity far from thermodynamic equilibrium. But we would also look for beings that need to "exert" themselves in some degree even to maintain their organic identity against the continual threat of being dissolved into their inanimate surroundings. Life elsewhere as well as here, in other words, could be identified as such only if it conforms in some way to what Michael Polanyi calls "the logic of achievement." How this understanding of life bears upon the question of whether ETs are religious will become clear shortly.[10]

Next, what do we mean by *intelligent* life, the special set of features for which SETI professes to be looking, and which we confidently think we could identify if we ever stumbled across it? First of all, if we find intelligent *life*, then it must be manifested in some sort of *striving*; and, second, if it is *intelligent* life, it must be the kind of striving that we associate with *a desire to understand and know*. If the desire for insight and truth is absent then there may be life—sentient and even conscious life—but not intelligent life. Any being that is not somehow striving to achieve some goal, even if this goal is simply that of surviving, is not alive; and any being whose striving does not include the search for insight and truth is not intelligent, at least in the sense that we humans minimally understand the term. SETI already tacitly assumes such a notion of "intelligence" when it searches the heavens for electromagnetic signals that only a technologically sophisticated, and similarly insight-seeking and truth-desiring source is sending out.[11]

Finally, what do we mean by *religion*? Let us understand by "religion" a specific kind of striving also. Before religion is anything else it is a manifestation of *life*, a specific kind of human life, striving toward a goal. Underneath all of its extravagant symbolic, ritualistic, doctrinal, ethical, and institutional foliage, religion is an expression of life— of intelligent life—striving, exploring, and hoping. Religion, we suggest, is intelligent life at perhaps its most intense level of striving.

The whole terrestrial religious endeavor may be thought of as a kind of "route finding," a quest for pathways that promise to carry us through the most intractable limits on life.[12] Even from our perch here on Earth, therefore, can we not identify at least some of the most severe limits that *all* other forms of intelligent life would inevitably have to face along with us? And in identifying these limits, would we not be placing ourselves and the Others within a common theological circle, one that would allow conversation with them in spite of wide ecological differences?

If the Others possess anything like what we call intelligent life we can reasonably expect to discover that extraterrestrials at least have the *capacity* for a religious mode of venturing. Since any possible Others we would ever encounter will be inhabitants of the same Big Bang universe that we belong to, the general features of this cosmos as made known to us by our terrestrial sciences will presumably also apply to them. We must expect to find, then, that any living, sentient, and intelligent beings will be subject to the transience and perishability characteristic of all things stationed on the slopes of entropy. They too would be subject to transience and eventual perishing. They, like us, would be subject to the threat of failure, and eventual nonbeing, that every living finite being has to confront.

We may conclude, then, that since all living and intelligent beings would experience the same basic physical limits on life that we do, a meaningful exchange about religious route finding through these limits could conceivably occur. For these Others, if they are truly striving centers, would also be in search of ways to transcend the limits on their particular forms of life. And if they are truly intelligent they would have an awareness of their possible nonbeing. They might even have, in other words, what theologian Paul Tillich calls "existential anxiety." Anxiety, the awareness of finitude, drives intelligent life to find a courage that can conquer the threat of nonbeing. In our human experience it is the quest for courage in the face of nonbeing that leads many of us to seek the foundational support of religious faith, and in some cases to an understanding of "God" as the source of courage to continue life's striving in the face of fate, death, guilt, and meaninglessness.[13] If any Others "out there" are alive and intelligent, it would not be surprising that they too need courage. If so, they would be no less potentially religious than we are.

What Implications Would the Discovery of Other Intelligent Beings Have on the Question of Cosmic Purpose?

Whether the universe has any "point" or "purpose" to it is a question that religions must always be concerned about, perhaps above all else. Religions, including our Abrahamic faith traditions, can put up with all kinds of particular scientific ideas as long as they do not contradict the sense that the whole of things is meaningful. They can survive the news that Earth is not the center of the universe, that humans are descended from simian ancestors, and that the universe is 14 billion years old. What they cannot put up with, however, is the suspicion that the whole of things is pointless.[14]

It is worth asking, therefore, how SETI might bear on the question of cosmic purpose and, by implication, on the meaning and mission of our own lives. Any serious theological reflection on cosmology takes the question of purpose to be both unavoidable and central. Generally speaking, *purpose* means the process of realizing a value. Consequently, to say that the universe has a purpose would be to imply that it is oriented toward the realization of something intrinsically good or valuable. Cosmic purpose does not have to imply a particular *telos* or end. Purpose is not identical with a predetermined plan or design, both of which tend to close off the future in a suffocating way. All we need in order to affirm cosmic purpose is an awareness that something of undeniable importance is going on in the universe, and that it is doing so in a way that is tied essentially and not just accidentally to the whole of the cosmos.

Accordingly, it would seem relevant to our understanding of what this universe is all about that we try to find out whether intelligent life is abundantly distributed throughout the cosmos, or, for that matter, whether it exists only here on Earth. Certainly the existence of ETI would force us to reexamine the claim by evolutionists such as Jacques Monod, Stephen Jay Gould, Richard Dawkins, and many others that life and intelligence are the results of utterly improbable, purely random statistical aberrations in an overwhelmingly lifeless and mindless universe. In this respect SETI would seem to have theological importance.

After all, *intelligence itself* is the most indubitable instance we have of intrinsic value. If you find yourself doubting or denying what we have just said, it is only because *you* are now at this moment spontaneously acknowledging the *value* of your own intelligence. It is impossible for you consistently to deny the intrinsic importance of your intelligence. By issuing judgments about the truth-status of the assertions we have just made, you have already demonstrated how deeply you treasure your own mind and its capacity to understand, criticize and know.

Now if what we have just said is correct—and you really can't doubt it without proving our point—then the existence of even one instance, or one planetary outpost, of intelligence in this vast universe might be enough to make the whole story that leads up to its existence a purposeful one, especially since that large cosmic story is insepara-ble from the emergence of intelligent life. With the help of physics and astrophysics you now understand how intricately your own intel-ligence is connected to the 14 billion-year cosmic story and to the physical features of the universe. So to assert that the universe is inher-ently purposeless seems arbitrary at best. To argue in complete seri-ousness that the cosmos is ultimately unintelligible, or even to entertain doubts about the purposiveness of this patently mind-bear-ing universe, would at this point in our scientific understanding of the cosmos seem to sabotage the very mind that is making such an asser-tion. An essentially mindless universe would be a purposeless one, but a universe in which intelligent life is an essential rather than acciden-tal property could hardly be called purposeless. And so, any future dis-covery that instances of intelligence occur abundantly in the universe could not help but place the burden of proof upon those who see no intrinsic connection between mind and the rest of nature.

Can Faith and Theology Provide Us with a Framework That Would Be Hospitable to, and Enthusiastic about, Meeting Up with ETI?

Theology is typically more responsive than predictive. Of course, a few prophetic voices can read the signs of the times and issue appro-priate warnings about what is to come. But, by and large, theology, undertaken as it is by finite and shortsighted humans, seldom accu-rately anticipates, much less prepares us for the crises that occur in connection with unprecedented events in human history or new discoveries in the realm of science. Indeed, most of the theological content of the dominant traditions comes from reaction to crises rather than anticipation of them. Undoubtedly, then, the shape theology would take on if we ever do encounter ETI cannot be accurately predicted here and now, but must await the event itself.

However, we suggest that the cosmic vision of Teilhard de Chardin as well as the process theology based on concepts of the philosopher Alfred North Whitehead are both already inherently open to being developed into a "theology after contact." Not the least of the reasons for their adaptability is that they have already enthusiastically embraced the Darwinian portrait of life as well as the notion that the entire universe is still coming into being. Although Teilhard reflected only occasionally on the possibility of ETI, keeping most of his speculation firmly anchored to our planet, the general thrust of his visionary writings is cosmic in scope. As such, the urge toward increasing complexity and consciousness, so evident to Teilhard in his surveys of the history of life on Earth, could also be a trend, he speculated, throughout the cosmos. For this famous Jesuit paleontologist (1881–1955), the "point" or purpose of the universe has something to do with the emergence and intensification of "complexity-consciousness." As physical complexity increases in the universe, Teilhard observes, so does consciousness. But, as he also acknowledges, the cosmic evolution of consciousness is still far from being finished. Here on Earth the envelope of "thought," which he called the "noosphere," is clothing our own planet in something like a "brain," and it is not inconceivable to him that parallel worlds of consciousness are evolving elsewhere.

Hence, it would not be difficult to graft onto Teilhard's openended story of increasing complexity-consciousness other instances of intelligent life that we may eventually find or that may find us. Theologically speaking, the whole universe is on an evolutionary journey into the mystery of God while God seeks to become increasingly more incarnate in the universe. Conceivably such an encounter of God and creation could take place on many planets throughout the universe as they burst forth into life, consciousness, freedom, and eventually the capacity for charity.[15]

Finally, contemporary "process theology," with its vision of cosmic purpose, is also expansive enough to accommodate the discovery of ETI. For the process philosopher Alfred North Whitehead and his theological followers, the purpose of the cosmos consists of its aim toward the intensification of beauty.[16] Because, at least for Whitehead, beauty is an intrinsic value, any process that leads toward its establishment could be called "teleological," at least in a loose sense. "Beauty," in Whitehead's thought, means the "harmony of contrasts" or the "ordering of novelty," many diverse instances of which have appeared in the evolution of the cosmos and in the emergence of life, mind, and culture in our terrestrial setting.

Intelligent life, however, is only one instance of cosmic beauty. We really have no idea of the many forms the cosmic aim toward bringing about beauty might assume within the totality of the universe. Perhaps, then, SETI has set its goals too narrowly for theology. What we call intelligent life might turn out to be too trivial a notion to capture what is already "out there," or the incalculable cosmic outcomes that may yet occur in the future of this unfinished universe (or multiverse). The notion of "beauty," however, is encompassing enough to anticipate a wide variety of cosmic evolutionary outcomes. As we explore the universe we should ask not only about the meaning of intelligence, but also about what the existence of beauty implies as far as the essential character of the whole universe is concerned. It is clear that the universe has always been dissatisfied with the monotony of the status quo, and so it has produced innumerable instances of ordered novelty. Perhaps the aim toward beauty, then, is enough to endow the universe with purpose—although it is not necessary for us to add that we would not be able to arrive at such a conclusion unless there were also intelligent subjects capable of enjoying it.

Notes

INTRODUCTION

1. An excellent, convenient, and highly recommended summary of the new cosmic story for readers of this book is that of Brian Thomas Swimme and Mary Evelyn Tucker, *Journey of the Universe* (New Haven: Yale University Press, 2011) accompanied by a helpful DVD.

CHAPTER 1:
IS FAITH OPPOSED TO SCIENCE?

1. Jerry A. Coyne, *Why Evolution Is True* (New York: Viking, 2009); Richard Dawkins, *The God Delusion* (New York: Houghton Mifflin, 2006); Sam Harris, *The End of Faith: Religion, Terror, and the Future of Reason* (New York: Norton, 2004); and *Letter to a Christian Nation* (New York: Knopf, 2007); Christopher Hitchens, *God Is Not Great: How Religion Poisons Everything* (New York: Hachette Book Group USA, 2007); Victor J. Stenger, *God: The Failed Hypothesis: How Science Shows That God Does Not Exist* (Amherst, NY: Prometheus, 2007); Carl Sagan, *The Demon-Haunted World: Science as a Candle in the Dark* (New York: Ballantine Books, 1997); Steven Weinberg, *Dreams of a Final Theory* (New York: Pantheon, 1992); Michael Shermer, *How We Believe: The Search for God in an Age of Science* (New York: W. H. Freeman, 2000); Owen Flanagan, *The Problem of the Soul: Two Visions of Mind and How to Reconcile Them* (New York: Basic Books, 2002).

2. Dawkins, *The God Delusion.*

3. See Ian Barbour, *Religion in an Age of Science* (San Francisco: HarperCollins, 1997), pp. 10–16.

4. Ibid., p. 15.

5. See especially Teilhard de Chardin, *The Human Phenomenon*, Sarah Appleton-Weber, trans. (Portland, OR: Sussex Academic Press, 1999).

6. Albert Einstein, *Ideas and Opinions* (New York: Modern Library, 1994), p. 46.

CHAPTER 2:
DOES SCIENCE RULE OUT A PERSONAL GOD?

1. In this book "conflict" is associated with scientism and scientific naturalism as defined in the introduction and chapter 1.

2. For examples of the conflict position see n. 1 in chapter 1.

3. See Charley Hardwick, *Events of Grace: Naturalism, Existentialism, and Theology* (Cambridge, UK: Cambridge University Press, 1996).

4. Steven Weinberg, *Dreams of a Final Theory* (New York: Pantheon, 1992), pp. 241–61.

5. Stephen Hawking and Leonard Modinow, *The Grand Design* (New York: Bantam, 2010).

6. See Daniel C. Dennett, *Consciousness Explained* (New York: Little, Brown, 1991).

7. Albert Einstein, *Ideas and Opinions* (New York: Bonanza Books, 1954), p. 11.

8. On almost every page of *The God Delusion*, for example, Dawkins switches back and forth between science and scientism, nearly always without alerting readers that he is doing so.

9. Richard Dawkins, "Tanner Lecture on Human Values" at Harvard University, 2003, cited by *Science and Theology News* online: http://www.stnews.org/archives/2004_february/web_x_richard.html.

10. Alex Rosenberg, "Why I Am a Naturalist," *New York Times*, September 17, 2011, http://opinionator.blogs.nytimes.com/ 2011/09/17 /why-i-am-a-naturalist/.

11. Paul K. Moser, *The Elusive God: Reorienting Religious Epistemology* (New York: Cambridge University Press, 2008), pp. 53–54.

12. Sam Harris, *Letter to a Christian Nation* (New York: Knopf, 2007), pp. 60–61.

13. Pierre Teilhard de Chardin, *How I Believe*, René Hague, trans. (New York: Harper & Row, 1969), p. 42.

14. See Wolfhart Pannenberg, *Faith and Reality*, John Maxwell, trans. (Philadelphia: Westminster, 1977); Wolfhart Pannenberg, *Toward a Theology of Nature*, Ted Peters, ed. (Louisville: Westminster/ John Knox, 1993); and Ted Peters, *God—The World's Future: Systematic Theology for a New Era*, 2nd ed. (Minneapolis: Fortress, 2000).

CHAPTER 3:
IS FAITH COMPATIBLE WITH EVOLUTION?

1. Two of the clearest examples of this conflict approach are Jerry A. Coyne, *Why Evolution Is True* (New York: Viking, 2009); and Richard Dawkins, *The God Delusion* (New York: Houghton Mifflin, 2006).

2. See John C. Greene, *Darwin and the Modern World View* (New York: Mentor Books, 1963), p. 44.

3. See Coyne, *Why Evolution Is True*, p. 22.

4. Richard Dawkins, *The Blind Watchmaker* (New York: Norton., 1986), p. 6.

5. Ibid.

6. Evolutionary scientists in their dialogue with "religion" often assume that all theologians are "creationists," unaware that the idea of "creation" is a highly nuanced notion in most theology. For one example of this mistake, see Niles Eldredge, *The Monkey Business* (New York: Washington Square Press, 1982), pp. 132–35.

7. Representatives of ID include Michael J. Behe, *Darwin's Black Box: The Biochemical Challenge to Evolution* (New York: Free Press, 1996); William Dembski, *Intelligent Design: The Bridge between Science and Theology* (Downers Grove, IL: InterVarsity, 1999); William A. Dembski, *The Design Inference: Eliminating Chance through Small Probabilities* (New York: Cambridge University Press, 1998); Phillip E. Johnson, *Darwin on Trial* (Downers Grove, IL: InterVarsity, 1991); James Porter Moreland, ed., *The Creation Hypothesis: Scientific Evidence for an Intelligent Designer* (Downers

Grove, IL: InterVarsity, 1994); Jonathan Wells, *Icons of Evolution: Science or Myth?* (Washington, DC: Regnery, 2000). For a critique of ID see Robert T. Pennock, *Tower of Babel: The Evidence against the New Creationism* (Cambridge, MA: MIT Press, 1999).

8. See L. Charles Birch, *Nature and God* (Philadelphia: Westminster, 1965), p. 103.

9. For a development of these ideas see John F. Haught, *The Cosmic Adventure* (New York: Paulist Press, 1984); *The Promise of Nature* (New York: Paulist Press, 1993); *God after Darwin: A Theology of Evolution* (Boulder, CO: Westview, 1999); and *Making Sense of Evolution* (Louisville: Westminster/John Knox, 2010).

CHAPTER 4:
DO MIRACLES REALLY HAPPEN?

1. Christopher Hitchens, *God Is Not Great: How Religion Poisons Everything* (New York: Hachette Book Group USA, 2007), p. 111.

2. Sam Harris, *Letter to a Christian Nation* (New York: Knopf, 2007), pp. 60–61.

3. A good representative of the contrast position is Rudolf Bultmann, "The New Testament and Mythology," in *Kerygma and Myth*, Hans Werner Bartsch, ed., Reginald Fuller, trans. (New York: Harper Torchbooks, 1961), pp. 1–44.

4. Peter W. Atkins, *The 2nd Law: Energy, Chaos, and Form* (New York: Scientific American Books, 1994), p. 200.

5. Our use of the analogy of grammar follows in part some ideas of the scientist and philosopher Michael Polanyi. See Michael Polanyi, *Knowing and Being*, Marjorie Grene, ed. (Chicago: University of Chicago Press, 1969); and Michael Polanyi, *The Tacit Dimension* (Garden City, NY: Doubleday Anchor, 1967), pp. 31–34.

CHAPTER 5:
WAS THE UNIVERSE CREATED?

1. Within specific galactic clusters there may be local movement of galaxies toward one another, but overall they move away from one another in the general expansion of space.

2. The most recent example of this speculation is Lawrence Krauss, *A Universe from Nothing: Why There Is Something Rather Than Nothing* (New York: Free Press, 2012).

3. Douglas Lackey, "The Big Bang and the Cosmological Argument," in *Religion and the Natural Sciences*, James Huchingson, ed. (New York: Harcourt Brace Jovanovich, 1993), p. 194.

4. Stephen Hawking, *A Brief History of Time* (New York: Bantam Books, 1988) pp. 140–41; see also Paul Davies, *The Mind of God: The Scientific Basis for a Rational World* (New York: Simon & Schuster, 1992), p. 66; and Stephen Hawking and Leonard Mlodinow, *The Grand Design* (New York: Bantam Books, 2010).

5. Lawrence Krauss, cited in n. 2 above, is one of several contemporary cosmologists who naïvely assume that science can talk about the meaning of "nothing" in a way that refutes the classic theological doctrine of *creatio ex nihilo*. In fact, to contrast, the theological meaning of "nothing" has *nothing* to do with what scientists like Krauss mean by the term.

6. Paul Tillich, *Systematic Theology*, 3 vols. (Chicago: University of Chicago Press, 1967), Vol. I, p. 209. For Tillich God is not a "cause" nor first in a causal series. Rather God is the Ground of All Causes.

7. It is no coincidence that most of the editorial endorsements of Krauss's new book, cited in n. 2, come from scholars closely associated with the New Atheism. Their over-riding agenda, no matter how complicated the science, is not scientific but theological.

8. See Ted Peters, "On Creating the Cosmos," in *Physics, Philosophy and Theology: A Common Quest for Understanding*, Robert J. Russell, William R. Stoeger, SJ, and George V. Coyne, SJ, eds. (Notre Dame, IN: University of Notre Dame Press, 1988), pp. 273–96.

9. Stanley Jaki, *Universe and Creed* (Milwaukee, WI: Marquette University Press), p. 27.

10. Teilhard de Chardin, *The Prayer of the Universe*, René Hague, trans. (New York: Harper & Row, 1973), pp. 120–21.

11. This thought is fundamental and pervasive in Pierre Teilhard de Chardin's book *Christianity and Evolution*, René Hague, trans. (New York: Harcourt Brace Jovanovich, 1969).

12. For the following see Michael Foster, "The Christian Doctrine of Creation and the Rise of Modern Science," *Mind* (1934): 446–68.

CHAPTER 6:
CAN CHEMISTRY ALONE EXPLAIN LIFE?

1. Francis H. C. Crick, *The Astonishing Hypothesis: The Scientific Search for the Soul* (New York: Charles Scribner's Sons, 1994), p. 3.

2. Francis H. C. Crick, *Of Molecules and Men* (Seattle: University of Washington Press, 1966), p. 10; see also J. D. Watson, *The Molecular Biology of the Gene* (New York: W. A. Benjamin, 1965), p. 67.

3. See Jacques Monod, *Chance and Necessity*, Austryn Wainhouse, trans. (New York: Vintage Books, 1972), p. 123.

4. See Michael Polanyi, *Personal Knowledge* (New York: Harper Torchbooks, 1964), and *The Tacit Dimension* (Garden City, NY: Doubleday Anchor, 1967).

5. Hans Jonas, *Mortality and Morality* (Evanston, IL: Northwestern University Press, 1996), pp. 60, 165–97.

6. See Stuart A. Kauffmann, *The Origins of Order: Self-Organization and Selection in Evolution* (New York: Oxford University Press, 1993).

7. In fact, however, information in another sense than we are using the term here is a factor even at the level of physics.

8. See Michael Polanyi, *Knowing and Being*, Marjorie Grene, ed. (Chicago: University of Chicago Press, 1969), pp. 225–39.

CHAPTER 7:
CAN SCIENCE EXPLAIN INTELLIGENCE?

1. See, for example, Paul M. Churchland, *The Engine of Reason, The Seat of the Soul: A Philosophical Journey into the Brain* (Cambridge, MA: MIT Press, 1995).

2. Daniel C. Dennett, *Consciousness Explained* (New York: Little, Brown, 1991), p. 33.

3. Francis Crick, *The Astonishing Hypothesis: The Scientific Search for the Soul* (New York: Charles Scribner's Sons, 1994), p. 3.

4. Ibid., p. 257.

5. See, for example, E. F. Schumacher, *A Guide for the Perplexed* (New York: Harper Colophon Books, 1978).

6. Crick, *The Astonishing Hypothesis*, p. 6.

7. Owen Flanagan, *The Problem of the Soul: Two Visions of Mind and How to Reconcile Them* (New York: Basic Books, 2002), p. 11.

8. Daniel Dennett, "Intelligent Thought," in *The Third Culture*, John Brockman, ed. (New York: Touchstone, 2006), p. 87.

9. Charles Darwin, "Letter to W. Graham, July 3rd, 1881," in *The Life and Letters of Charles Darwin*, Francis Darwin, ed. (New York: Basic Books, 1959), p. 285.

10. Richard Rorty, "Untruth and Consequences," *New Republic*, July 31, 1995, 32–36. References here to both Darwin and Rorty appear in an online essay entitled "Darwin, Mind and Meaning" (1996) by Alvin Plantinga: http://idwww.ucsb.edu/fscf/library/plantinga/dennett.html.

11. For a book-length response to this question see John F. Haught, *Is Nature Enough? Meaning and Truth in the Age of Science* (Cambridge, UK: Cambridge University Press, 2006).

12. See ibid., pp. 209–15.

13. Peter W. Atkins, *The 2nd Law: Energy, Chaos, and Form* (New York: Scientific American Books, 1994), p. 200; Alex Rosenberg, "Why I Am a Naturalist," *New York Times*, September 17, 2011; Jerry A. Coyne, *Why Evolution Is True* (New York: Viking, 2009); Steven Weinberg, *Dreams of a Final Theory* (New York: Pantheon Books, 1992), pp. 241–61.

14. This theme of specialists generalizing is that of the psychiatrist Viktor Frankl: http://www.archive.org/stream/godandtheunconsc 027883mbp/godandtheunconsc027883mbp_djvu.txt.

15. One of most unembarrassed attempts to "unify" all human knowledge in terms of a scientific specialist's materialist metaphysics is E. O. Wilson's *Consilience: The Unity of Knowledge* (New York: Knopf, 1998).

16. These thoughts are inspired in great measure by Pierre Teilhard de Chardin, *The Human Phenomenon*, Sarah Appleton-Weber, trans. (Portland, OR: Sussex Academic Press, 1999).

CHAPTER 8:
CAN WE BE GOOD WITHOUT GOD?

1. For a more neurological and less evolutionary, but still naturalistic, account of morality see Sam Harris, *The Moral Landscape: How Science Can Determine Human Values* (New York: Free Press, 2010).

2. See, for example, Matt Ridley, *The Origins of Virtue: Human Instincts and the Evolution of Cooperation* (New York: Penguin Books, 1998).

3. See Robert Wright, *The Moral Animal: Evolutionary Psychology and Everyday Life* (New York: Pantheon, 1994).

4. Ridley, *The Origins of Virtue*, p. 12.

5. For details see George C. Williams, *Adaptation and Natural Selection: A Critique of Some Current Evolutionary Thought* (Princeton, NJ: Princeton University Press, 1996); William D. Hamilton, "The Genetical Evolution of Social Behavior," *Journal of Theoretical Biology* 7 (1964): 1–52; John Maynard Smith, *The Evolution of Sex* (New York: Cambridge University Press, 1978); Robert L. Trivers, *Social Evolution* (Menlo Park, CA: Benjamin Cummings, 1985); Richard D. Alexander, *Darwinism and Human Affairs* (Seattle: University of Washington Press, 1979); see also Jerome H. Barkow, Leda Cosmides, and John Tooby, eds., *The Adapted Mind: Evolutionary Psychology and the Generation of Culture* (New York: Oxford University Press, 1992). For a more detailed discussion of this chapter's topic see John F. Haught, *Is*

Nature Enough: Meaning and Truth in the Age of Science (Cambridge, UK: Cambridge University Press, 2006), and *Deeper Than Darwin: The Prospect for Religion in the Age of Evolution* (Boulder, CO: Westview, 2003).

6. Discussions of this example refer readers to John Hoogland, *The Black-Tailed Prairie Dog: Social Life of a Burrowing Mammal* (Chicago: University of Chicago Press, 1995).

7. See especially Christopher Hitchens, *God Is Not Great: How Religion Poisons Everything* (New York: Hachette Book Group USA, 2007).

8. Jacques Monod, *Chance and Necessity*, Austryn Wainhouse, trans. (New York: Vintage Books, 1972), pp. 175–80.

9. Cited by William James in "The Will to Believe," in *The Will to Believe, and Other Essays in Popular Philosophy* (New York: Longmans, Green, and Co., 1931).

10. As implied in the title of his book *God Is Not Great.*

11. See, for example, Richard Dawkins, *The God Delusion* (New York: Houghton Mifflin, 2006), pp. 220ff.

12. For the following see James W. Fowler, *Stages of Faith: The Psychology of Human Development and the Quest for Meaning* (San Francisco: Harper & Row, 1981); and Michael Barnes, *Stages of Thought: The Co-evolution of Religious Thought and Science* (New York: Oxford University Press, 2000).

13. See, for example, Barbara King, *Evolving God: A Provocative View on the Origins of Religion* (New York: Doubleday, 2007).

14. Again, see Barnes, *Stages of Thought.*

15. For this analogy see Holmes Rolston III, *Science and Religion: A Critical Survey* (Philadelphia: Templeton Foundation Press, 2006), p. 108.

16. Pierre Teilhard de Chardin, *Activation of Energy*, René Hague, trans. (New York: Harcourt Brace Jovanovich, 1970), pp. 229–44.

17. Pierre Teilhard de Chardin, *Human Energy*, J. M. Cohen, trans. (New York: Harvest Books/Harcourt Brace Jovanovich, 1962), p. 29.

18. See ibid. For this interpretation of morality, convergence is deeply indebted to countless suggestions of Teilhard de Chardin throughout his large body of writings.

CHAPTER 9:
ARE WE SPECIAL?

1. Freeman Dyson, *Disturbing the Universe* (New York: Harper & Row, 1979), p. 250.

2. The best available discussion of AP is still that of John Barrow and Frank Tipler, *The Anthropic Cosmological Principle* (Oxford, UK: Clarendon Press, 1986).

3. Martin Rees, *Just Six Numbers: The Deep Forces That Shape the Universe* (New York: Basic Books, 2000); and Martin Rees, *Our Cosmic Habitat* (Princeton, NJ: Princeton University Press, 2001).

4. See the similar point made by Nicholas Lash, "Observation, Revelation, and the Posterity of Noah," in *Physics, Philosophy and Theology*, Robert J. Russell, William Stoeger, SJ, and George Coyne, SJ, eds. (Notre Dame, IN: University of Notre Dame Press, 1988), p. 211.

5. See, for example, Rees, *Our Cosmic Habitat.*

6. Strictly speaking, this could be called the "Narrative Cosmological Principle," but we refer to it, somewhat imprecisely, as NAP to preserve the parallelism with TAP and NAP.

7. This is highly simplified version of the worldview that Bernard Lonergan calls "Emergent Probability" in *Insight: A Study of Human Understanding*, 3rd ed. (New York: Philosophical Library, 1970).

CHAPTER 10:
IS THERE LIFE AFTER DEATH?

1. Owen Flanagan, *The Problem of the Soul: Two Visions of Mind and How to Reconcile Them* (New York: Basic Books, 2002), pp. 167–68.

2. Ibid., pp. ix–x.

3. Examples of this lenient evolutionary perspective are Pascal Boyer, *Religion Explained: The Evolutionary Origins of Religious Thought* (New York: Basic Books, 2001); Walter Burkert, *Creation of the Sacred: Tracks of Biology in Early Religions* (Cambridge, MA: Harvard University Press, 1996); Scott Atran, *In Gods We Trust: The*

Evolutionary Landscape of Religion (New York: Oxford University Press, 2002); and Loyal Rue, *By the Grace of Guile: The Role of Deception in Natural History and Human Affairs* (New York: Oxford University Press, 1994).

4. William James, *Pragmatism* (Cleveland: Meridian, 1964), p. 76.

5. For development of this point see John Hick, *The Fifth Dimension: An Exploration of the Spiritual Realm* (Oxford, UK: Oneworld, 1999); and John F. Haught, *Is Nature Enough: Meaning and Truth in the Age of Science* (Cambridge, UK: Cambridge University Press, 2006.)

6. Albert Camus, *The Myth of Sisyphus, and Other Essays*, Justin O'Brien, trans. (New York: Knopf, 1955), pp. 21, 88–91.

7. Steven Weinberg, *Dreams of a Final Theory* (New York: Pantheon, 1992), p. 256.

8. Ibid., pp. 255, 260.

9. Hick, *The Fifth Dimension*, p. 22.

10. Ibid., p. 24.

11. Alfred North Whitehead, *Science and the Modern World* (New York: Free Press, 1967), pp. 191–92.

12. For elaboration see Alfred North Whitehead, *Process and Reality*, corr. ed., David Ray Griffin and Donald W. Sherburne, eds. (New York: Free Press, 1968), pp. 29, 34–51, 60, 81–82, 86–104, 340–51; and Alfred North Whitehead, "Immortality," in *The Philosophy of Alfred North Whitehead*, Paul A. Schillp, ed. (Evanston and Chicago: Northwestern University Press, 1941), pp. 682–700. See also Charles Hartshorne, *The Logic of Perfection* (Lasalle, IL: Open Court, 1962), pp. 250; 24–62.

13. Reinhold Niebuhr, "Introduction" to William James, *The Varieties of Religious Experience* (New York: Collier, 1961), p. 7.

14. See n. 12 above.

CHAPTER 11:
DOES THE UNIVERSE HAVE A PURPOSE?

1. Richard Lewontin, "Billions and Billions of Demons," *New York Review of Books*, January 9, 1997, 31.

2. Steven Weinberg, *The First Three Minutes* (New York: Basic Books, 1977), pp. 144.

3. John Polkinghorne, "Creation and the Structure of the Physical World," *Theology Today*, 44 (April 1987), 53–68; Freeman Dyson, *Disturbing the Universe* (New York: Harper & Row, 1979); Paul Davies, *The Mind of God: The Scientific Basis for a Rational World* (New York: Simon & Schuster, 1992).

4. "Evolution and the Foundation of Ethics," in *Science, Technology and Social Progress*, Steven L. Goldman, ed. (Bethlehem, PA: Lehigh University Press, 1989), p. 261.

5. James Jeans, *The Mysterious Universe*, rev. ed. (New York: Macmillan, 1948), pp. 15–16 (first published in 1930).

6. Stephen Jay Gould, *Ever Since Darwin* (New York: Norton), p. 13.

7. E. D. Klemke, "Living without Appeal," in *The Meaning of Life* (New York: Oxford University Press, 1981), pp. 169–72.

8. The most accessible introduction to these ideas is Pierre Teilhard de Chardin, *The Future of Man*, Norman Denny, trans. (New York: Harper & Row, 1964).

9. See Pierre Teilhard de Chardin, *Human Energy*, J. M. Cohen, trans. (New York: Harcourt Brace Jovanovich, 1969), p. 25.

CHAPTER 12:
WHAT IF EXTRATERRESTRIALS EXIST?

This chapter is adapted from John F. Haught, "Theology after Contact: Religion and Extra-Terrestrial Intelligent Life," *Cosmic Questions* (New York: New York Academy of Sciences Press, 2001), pp. 296–308.

1. See Michael J. Crowe, *The Extraterrestrial Life Debate 1750–1900* (Cambridge, UK: Cambridge University Press, 1986); Stephen J. Dick, *Plurality of Worlds: The Origins of the Extraterrestrial Life Debate from Democritus to Kant* (Cambridge, UK: Cambridge University Press, 1982); Ted Peters, "Exo-Theology: Speculations on Extraterrestrial Life," in *The Gods Have Landed: New Religions from Other Worlds*, James R. Lewis, ed. (Albany: State University of New York Press, 1995), pp. 187–206.

2. See H. Richard Niebuhr, *Radical Monotheism and Western Culture* (London: Faber and Faber, 1943).

3. Roch Kereszty, as quoted by Thomas F. O'Meara, "Extraterrestrial Intelligent Life," *Theological Studies* 60 (March 1999): 29.

4. *Summa Theologica* I, 48, ad 2.

5. The term *exo-theology* (a take-off on "exo-biology," which studies the prospects of life outside of our planet) is used by Peters, "Exo-Theology," p. 188.

6. Quoted by Stephen J. Dick, *Life on Other Worlds: The 20th-Century Extraterrestrial Life Debate* (Cambridge, UK: Cambridge University Press, 1998), p. 194.

7. Mary Russell, *The Sparrow* (New York: Fawcett Columbine, 1996).

8. This question has been often raised by Thomas Berry. See his book *Dream of the Earth* (San Francisco: Sierra Club Books), p. 11.

9. See Michael Polanyi, *Personal Knowledge: Towards a Post-Critical Philosophy* (New York and Evanston: Harper & Row, 1958), pp. 327, 344.

10. Ibid., pp. 327–46.

11. For a thorough study of what it means to be "intelligent," see Bernard Lonergan, *Insight: A Study of Human Understanding*, 3rd ed. (New York: Philosophical Library, 1970).

12. John Bowker, *Is Anybody Out There?* (Westminster, MD: Christian Classics, 1988), pp. 9–18, 112–43.

13. Paul Tillich, *The Courage to Be* (New Haven: Yale University Press, 1952), pp. 40–45.

14. See W. T. Stace, "Man against Darkness," *Atlantic Monthly*, September 1948, 54.

15. See Pierre Teilhard de Chardin, *Activation of Energy*, René Hague, trans. (New York: Harcourt Brace Jovanovich, 1970), pp. 99–127. In 1944 Teilhard wrote that the hypothesis of other planets inhabited by intelligent beings has a "positive likelihood," in which case "the phenomenon of life and more particularly the phenomenon of man lose something of their disturbing loneness" (p. 127). There may be many "noospheres" or "thinking planets." "It is almost more than our minds can dare to face," Teilhard continues, but the evolu-

tionary tendency toward complexification and centration might well have a "cosmic" scope. Yet "there can still be only a single Omega," that is, a single transcendent Reality whose being attracts and enfolds the entire universe (p. 127).

16. See Alfred North Whitehead, *Adventures of Ideas* (New York: Free Press, 1967), esp. p. 265.

Index

191